THE OAKWOOD LIBRARY OF RAILWAY HISTORY   OL170

The Maryport & Carlisle Railway

by
Robert Western

© Oakwood Press & Robert Western 2023

Published by Oakwood Press, an imprint of Stenlake Publishing Ltd, 54-58 Mill Square, Catrine, KA5 6RD *Tel:* 01290 551122 *Website:* www.stenlake.co.uk

British Library Cataloguing in Publication Data
A Record for this book is available from the British Library
ISBN 978 0 85361 768 6

Printed by Blissetts, Unit 1, Shield Drive, West Cross Industrial Park, TW8 9EX

All rights reserved. No part of this book may be reproduced or transmitted in any form or by any means, electronic or mechanical, including photocopying, recording or by any information storage and retrieval system, without permission from the Publisher in writing.

By the same author
The Ingleton Branch, Oakwood Press, 1990 (Revised Edition, 2018)
  (First published as *The Lowgill Branch*, Oakwood, 1971)
The Eden Valley Railway, Oakwood Press, 1997 (Revised Edition, 2014)
The Cockermouth Keswick and Penrith Railway, Oakwood Press, 2001
  (Revised Edition, 2007)
The Coniston Railway, Oakwood Press, 2007
The Kendal & Windermere Railway, Oakwood Press, 2012
The Mansfield Railway, Oakwood Press, 2019
The Mansfield-Southwell-Rolleston Railway, Oakwood Press, 2021

Many photographs of trains in M&CR days are taken in close proximity to Carlisle Citadel station. Here 0-6-0 No. 14 has been pressed into service on a passenger train. The locomotive is in its rebuilt form with a domed boiler. *Author's Collection*

Title page: Another view of a M&CR passenger train departing Carlisle Citadel, this time taken a little closer to the station. The train engine is rather more usual motive power in the form of 2-4-0 No. 13 which was built at Maryport Works in 1873. We see it here in its rebuilt form. *Author's Collection*

Front cover: The M&CR took delivery of No. 12 in 1865. This 4-2-0 passenger locomotive was built to the Crampton patent by Tulk & Ley of Lowca and is reproduced here from an original C. Hamilton Ellis carriage print. The locomotive was rebuilt as a 2-2-2 in 1860, No. 12 then went on to give a further 10 years service to the railway. *Author's Collection*

Rear cover: The Railway Clearing House map of 1917 showing the Maryport & Carlisle and surrounding railways. *Oakwood Collection*

Contents

	Preamble	5
Chapter One	**Beginnings, 1836-1844** *The company is set up – Stephenson arranges a survey – A Bill and subsequent Act – Building commences with some sections opened – Three further Acts*	6
Chapter Two	**The line is completed, 1845-1850** *The line is completed – A crisis of management – Issues with the Lancaster & Carlisle – George Hudson, 'The Railway King' takes over – 'Strange and stirring times at Crown Street Station' – National criticism of the company's behaviour*	23
Chapter Three	**Pulling together, 1851-1860** *Another Act – Use of Citadel Station – Fare revisions – Peace with the Lancaster & Carlisle – A further Act*	40
Chapter Four	**An increase in prosperity and further projects, 1861-1871** *Plans for expansion – The shadow of a threat*.......................	51
Chapter Five	**Improvements in operations, 1872-1900** *A serious accident – Depression in the coal and ore trade*	61
Chapter Six	**The company's final years, 1900-1923** *The last locomotive is built in the company's works – A change to the liveries – Further decline in some sectors of the revenue – The changes following World War I – The demise of the company*	65
Chapter Seven	**Description of the line**	75
Chapter Eight	**Locomotives and rolling stock**	98
Appendix One	**Opening sequence of the Maryport & Carlisle**	117
Appendix Two	**Locomotive Superintendents**	117
Appendix Three	**Opening and closure dates to passengers**.................	118
	Sources and thanks	119
	Index...	120

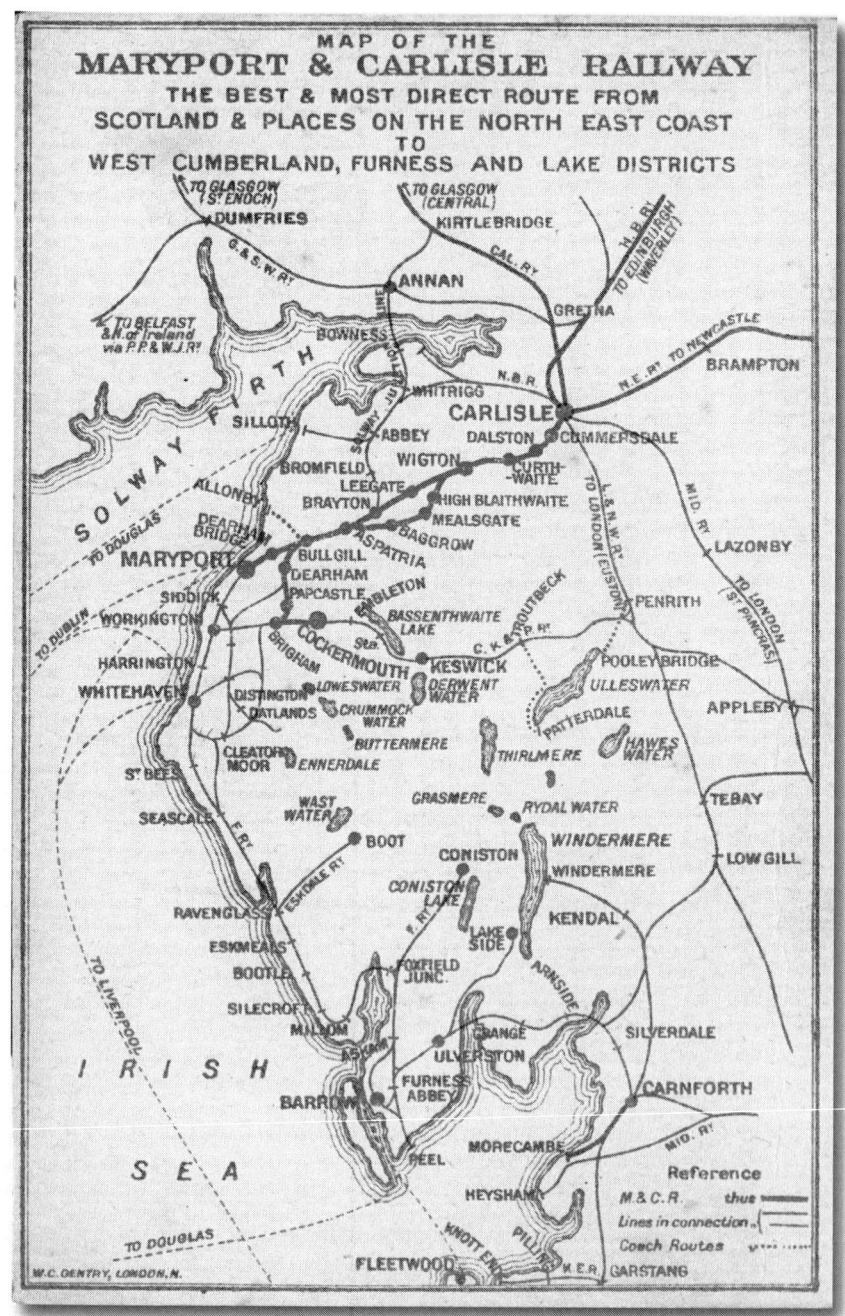

A promotional map showing the M&CR and connecting routes. *John Alsop Collection*

Preamble

The early part of the 19th century saw a huge surge in the demand for coal and other resources in order to power the rapidly developing industrial requirements. Transporting these commodities had originally been done using carts pulled by horses and sometimes oxen, then by the widely developed canal system which improved transportation even though it could be slow and cumbersome. The practical advantages of railways created opportunities for setting up companies with the prime purpose of transporting coal, lime and other chemicals which had a part to play, not least in the production of iron and later steel, the uses for which were becoming extensive. In addition it was recognised there was revenue to be made by carrying passengers.

A group of individuals in the north-west of Cumberland realised this soon after railway development had reached a stage when it could be seen that it would become widely available. A scheme was proposed whereby local collieries would be easily serviced and also there would be the opportunity to develop the shipping of coal to Ireland. One of the leaders in the field, George Stephenson, was enlisted to organise a survey of a route.

The outcome was that the Maryport & Carlisle Railway (M&CR) was comparatively early on the scene as far as the development of the railway system was concerned. Initially this project certainly had the main purpose of serving some of the coalfields of Cumberland and this is apparent in the priority when building commenced. The business prospects looked promising and eventually proved to be so. This driving force is evident and there was the additional objective of linking east and west in this part of the country. There was also much to be gained from carrying passengers and this too became an important element in the company's planning.

Yet it becomes clear that in the early days, with little experience, there was much to be learned and enthusiasm and drive did not match some of the expertise required. To some extent this is seen in the number of Bills and subsequent Acts of Parliament which resulted in, at one stage, a leading contemporary observer on railway matters commenting that the company 'proceeded as though Acts of Parliament were waste paper and ignored'.

The line took considerably longer to build than planned, but it eventually emerged as a successful venture which would remain viable and determined. In the long run, it maintained its independence until finally it was left with no option and it passed into history with the company being absorbed into the London, Midland & Scottish Railway (LMS) at the Grouping of 1923.

Chapter One

Beginnings, 1836-1844

1836

On Tuesday 3rd May, George Stephenson sat at his desk in 16 Duke Street, Westminster, to write a letter in readiness for a meeting of a group planning to build a railway from Maryport to Carlisle. 'Gentlemen, I now beg to inform you that my assistant, Mr Hall, having arrived in London, has laid before me a full account of the investigation which he has made of the Country between Maryport and Carlisle …' In the letter he confirms that the report of the work carried out will serve, when it is read, to substantiate that the route being planned 'will be a good one'. He believes the cost will be £200,000 and points out that it will be 'favourable for locomotive engines because the gradients will enable this to be so and also because there are few curves and this will allow for high velocities'. Further, he feels it will be possible to carry coal 'at a low rate'. The length of the line will be 28 miles and he recommends a double line through the 'mineral district' on the Maryport side of the ridge. Stephenson would visit the area later in the year.

Contemporary reports lead to the conclusion that three years earlier the main catalyst for a movement to build a railway for Maryport was the scheme for a railway between Newcastle and Carlisle. When the Newcastle & Carlisle Railway opened the first section of its line between Hexham and Blaydon, with the prospect of the link between the two places in its title soon to be completed, it inspired others to aspire to serving Maryport similarly. One such person was Capt. Sir Humphrey le Fleming Senhouse RN, a very distinguished member of Her Majesty's Navy. He owned what latterly became known as Steelfield Hall near Gosforth and had gained quite a reputation in the area. When considering the prospects of the Newcastle & Carlisle, he had clearly perceived the advantages such a railway would bring and was convinced a similar facility should be made available to Maryport.

The opportunity to speak to a wide audience about his views came, when in December 1834, a dinner was held in his honour. In his speech he made it clear that in his view extending the line of the Newcastle & Carlisle to Maryport would 'bring great advantages to the town and harbour'. His point of view was that the prospect of carrying goods over land rather than the necessity of taking them by sea, would have great advantages. At one point 'speaking as a sailor' he commented, 'Let us see then whether steam while it gives great danger to our needs at sea, will not give us greater facility at home' and stated that he would keenly support any project to achieve this objective. His words obviously fired the imagination of his listeners because a number of them determined to get together and act on what he had said.

It transpired that the suggestion which had been made to continue the Newcastle & Carlisle to Maryport was not seen as a practical one. So the group set about planning their own line between Maryport and Carlisle and approached George Stephenson to survey a suitable route for such a line. He agreed to arrange this and Mr Hall was sent off to Cumberland.

On Monday 16th May there was a meeting of initial subscribers to receive and consider the report Stephenson had sent and also to elect directors. Sir Wilfrid Lawson, called upon to act as Chairman for this meeting, informed those present that 'Stephenson's Report and the Draft Prospectus were ready' and proposed 'these be printed for circulation along with the Lythographic Plans for the line'. This was readily agreed.

The Prospectus was headed 'An Exposition of the Traffic Actual and Prospective on the line of the Maryport and Carlisle Railway'. It emphasised the importance of the various commodities that would be transported by the line; coal in particular, but also lime, stone and slate. A point was made about the significance of linking up in some way with the Newcastle & Carlisle Railway and in so doing, linking east and west. It was argued, based on the report Stephenson had sent, that the line 'could be built extremely cheaply'. In addition it was stated that the line would be so profitable that there could well be a dividend of 18¾ per cent. It was even suggested that as well as improving trade with Ireland, it could enhance trade with America. The group was very confident of its success. When it came to projecting annual receipts the figure was presented as a very precise £35,544 16s. 1d. What is perhaps interesting is that it was reckoned more than half of this amount would come from carrying passengers who 'would be carried to the Sea Coast for bathing, to Liverpool, Whitehaven, the Isle of Man and Ireland'. Stephenson's report was included.

A committee of management and 26 directors were elected and given power and authority in the name of the shareholders. For a small company this might seem to be a large number of directors and would prove to be something of an encumbrance in later years. On occasions there were meetings at which the directors outnumbered the shareholders. The first Chairman appointed for the company was J.P. Senhouse who would hold this position for six years. The necessary measures for obtaining an Act in the next session of Parliament for the incorporation of the company were then proposed and approved. It was agreed that any five of the directors would form a quorum.

There was a clear feeling that in the light of the Engineer's report and projections for revenue and income, the undertaking would be 'speedily executed' and prove to be a sure and safe investment. With the figure of £200,000 projected it was agreed that shares would be £50 each with a deposit of £2 per share.

In further deliberations it was said that the proposed line of the railway would 'unite the flourishing and manufacturing town of Carlisle with the seaport town of Maryport and would pass through Wigton and close to Dalston'. The objective stated was the move to join the railway already in progress between Newcastle and Carlisle and 'to open a route between the German Ocean [the North Sea] and the Irish Sea'.

This was followed up with further action and an announcement in the *Carlisle Journal* on 22nd October:

> Notice is given that Application is to be made to Parliament in the next session for leave to bring a Bill in order to obtain an Act for making and maintaining a Railway or Railways to be called the Maryport and Carlisle Railway.

It goes on to give the details. In the same edition of the newspaper there is a letter from George Stephenson. This is addressed to 'The Directors' but given they are no doubt aware of the plans without reading them in a newspaper, it is possibly aimed to bring attention to a wider audience and those who might be ready to be supporters of the scheme. Stephenson writes that he has now 'minutely examined the route' and is confident of the proposals. He gives the origin of the letter not as his London office but Alston Grange (12th October) and so clearly he has come to the locality to make the 'minute examination'. At one point the letter gives a reassurance that the line will not cause 'annoyance to Gentlemen's pleasure grounds', perhaps with the intention of avoiding powerful opposition and the hope of winning over supporters with influence.

1837

At a meeting on 6th May it was stated that a report of the Committee of the House of Commons upon the Bill which was by now in the House of Lords, had been published. It outlined a number of elements: the proposed capital was £180,000 and the company would be empowered to raise by loan £60,000; the number of shares subscribed would be £150,350 (3,007 at £50 each); the deposits paid being £2 each on 2,530 shares.

It noted that 'the existing conveyance is insufficient for the transit of passengers and goods and that much advantage would result for agricultural, commercial and manufacturing and mining interests from a cheaper and more rapid conveyance and communication between the proposed termini'. It was now predicted that the number of passengers would be about 231,256 per annum and the weight of goods 12,480 tons per annum and these would include cotton, flax, groceries and agricultural items. The income anticipated was £30,368 and this would be made up of: passengers £15,545 7s. 3d. and goods £14,817 12s. 9d.

It was also noted that the proposed railway 'is a complete and integral line between the termini specified but it is intended to connect it with the Newcastle & Carlisle Railway in order to achieve a continuous communication by the railway from the German Ocean to the Irish Sea together with a proposed railway from Maryport to Whitehaven' and that there would be 'no competing lines in progress or in contemplation'. There were no engineering problems anticipated and no need for assistant engines. The gradients were favourable as were the radii of the curves. The line would be 28 miles and 1 chain and there would be no branches. Furthermore there would be no intention 'to pass on a level any turnpike road', although there was the proposal:

... to pass on two highways, one leading from Wigton to Abbey Holme and one leading from Wigton to Staveling Stone 'neither cannot be passed by sinking the railway below without making inclined planes and going below the bed of the River Wiza which is within 50 yards of the projected line so that the railway would be subjected to be overflowed and the present roads could not be taken over the railway without causing steep ascents and descents and because the two roads are not much used and because there will be a station between them the speed of the engines at that point will be relatively diminished.

The engineers who examined in support of the Bill were 'G. Stephenson Esq. and William Snooke Hall'. It was pointed out that no petition had been presented against the Bill. Listed among the shareholders were two who had a very significant sum compared with the rest. Sir Wilfrid Lawson had purchased 315 and 'H. Senhouse' acquired 400. The total number of shares purchased was 1,890 at a cost of £94,500. The Bill went forward.

The name George Stephenson echoes down many railway projects in this era and he was renowned for his work and expertise. His name appearing on the Bill when it went before the Commons would probably have carried a great deal of weight.

The resulting Act, Vict. cap. ci, is dated 12th July, 1837. It is extremely lengthy and runs to over 106 pages with these being divided into 209 sections. The opening paragraph spells out the main objectives and reads as follows (italics as in the document):

> An Act for making a Railway from the Town and Port of *Maryport* to the Borough of Carlisle to be called The Maryport and Carlisle *Railway*. Whereas the making of a Railway from the Town and Port of *Maryport* to the Borough of *Carlisle* in the County of *Cumberland* there to join the *Newcastle-upon-Tyne* and *Carlisle* Railway, would be productive of great Advantages to the Agricultural, Manufacturing, Mining and Commercial Interests of the said County and the adjoining County of *Northumberland* and to the Public in general, by affording great additional Facilities for the Transit of Passengers, Merchandise, and Minerals within the said County of *Cumberland* and, as well as for the Home Consumption as for Exportation or Shipment to *Ireland* and the Western Coast of *England* by forming in conjunction with the *Newcastle-upon-Tyne* and *Carlisle* Railway and the *Brandlings* Junction Railway [in County Durham] once complete and continuous Line of Railway Communication from the *German* Ocean to the *Irish Sea*. And whereas the several persons herein after mentioned are linking their own Costs and Charges to carry into execution the said Undertaking; but the same cannot be effected without the Authority of Parliament; May it please Your Majesty that it may be enacted; and it be enacted by the Queen's Most Excellent Majesty.

The Act goes on to name those who have signed up to the undertaking. The list is a very long one with the first two names being Sir Wilfrid Lawson and Sir Humphrey le Fleming Senhouse. Much of the detail in the opening sections refers to the conditions relating to the impact on roads and the regulations appropriate to how the company will need to act in, for example, not causing inconvenience to those who use or own them.

In section LXXIII there is a condition which states that any minerals under the land purchased to build the line will not become the property of the company

ANNO PRIMO

VICTORIÆ REGINÆ.

✳✳✳

Cap. ci.

An Act for making a Railway from the Town and Port of *Maryport* to the Borough of *Carlisle*, to be called "The *Maryport* and *Carlisle* Railway."
[12th *July* 1837.]

WHEREAS the making of a Railway from the Town and Port of *Maryport* to the Borough of *Carlisle* in the County of *Cumberland*, there to join the *Newcastle-upon-Tyne* and *Carlisle* Railway, would be productive of great Advantages to the Agricultural, Manufacturing, Mining, and Commercial Interests of the said County and the adjoining County of *Northumberland*, and to the Public in general, by affording great additional Facilities for the Transit of Passengers, Merchandize, and Minerals within the said County of *Cumberland*, as well for Home Consumption as for Exportation or Shipment to *Ireland*, *Scotland*, and other Places; and the said Railway would also facilitate the Communication between the Continent of *Europe* and *Ireland* and the Western Coast of *England* by forming, in conjunction with the said *Newcastle-upon-Tyne* and *Carlisle* Railway and the *Brandlings* Junction Railway, One complete and continuous Line of Railway Communication from the *German* Ocean to the *Irish* Sea: And whereas the several Persons herein-after named are willing, at their own Costs and Charges, to carry into execution the said Undertaking; but the same cannot be effected without the Authority of Parliament: May it therefore please Your Majesty that it may be enacted; and be it enacted by the Queen's

[*Local.*]   40 *Q*   most

and also limiting how much of them can be removed in order to build the line. Section LXXXIX specifies that the company can raise, as was proposed in the Bill, up to £180,000 in shares of £50 each.

A significant condition which the company would have to work hard to satisfy is listed in section LXXIII, namely that completion of the line must be within seven years.

Much of the latter part of the Act deals with matters relating to shares and shareholding, together with procedures for holding meetings, and goes into considerable detail on these aspects. As time went by there would be some disquiet and altercations between the directors and the shareholders about matters of procedure.

A decision had been made that the coat of arms for the company would include those of Senhouse and Lawson, quartered with those of Maryport, so reflecting for some the 'feudal element' of the line! There is a passing reference that during the year the practice of 'cutting the first sod' was carried out by John Wood, Robert Kitson and Dr Rae. This procedure was usually accompanied by a good deal of celebration but none is mentioned and the three persons involved do not feature later.

Maryport & Carlisle Railway coat of arms.

1838

The directors set up a planning meeting for Monday 2nd April and in the light of this a notice appeared in the local press on Saturday 10th March inviting sealed tenders for various contracts for the first section of the line.

The first was the 'Maryport contract'. This related to a line from South Quay at Maryport and terminating in the township of Birkby – a length of 2 miles and 5 furlongs. There would be a requirement to maintain the track for one year. The contractor would be required to excavate all the embankments, erect fences, provide road bridges, culverts and any other works and also to provide all the materials. The contractor was not, however, required to supply the rails, chairs, blocks, sleepers, spikes and keys.

The second was the 'Crosby contract' to commence at the termination of the Maryport contract and terminate in the parish of Gilcrux. This would be 2½ miles with the same conditions being applied.

The third was the 'Gilcrux contract' to commence at the termination of the previous contract. This would terminate at the crossing on the road from Oughterside to Plumbland in the township of Arkleby, a section of 2 miles and 1 furlong. This tender would include wooden bridges to be erected over the River Ellen with a 40ft span.

Those wishing to be considered were informed that the specifications would be ready by Monday 12th March. There was a rider to all this because contractors were informed that they would have to provide all temporary rails, wagons and materials for their own use. There was also a caveat. This stated that those whose tenders were accepted would be required to enter into bonds with two securities for the due performance of their contracts in a penalty of not less than 10 per cent on the gross sum contracted for.

Things were beginning to move and at the same time as this notice went out there was a call on proprietors of £5 per share to be paid to the treasurer at Maryport before 2nd April. The contract for the work was awarded to Blackstock & McKay. A significant event, vital to the Maryport & Carlisle in the days ahead, was the opening of the Newcastle & Carlisle Railway on 18th June. The relationship between the two companies would fluctuate with changing circumstances.

1839

Although George Stephenson was initially involved with the Maryport & Carlisle project it was only at the outset. In 1839 he decided to stand down and John Blackmore was appointed in his place. Quite why Stephenson decided to step down is not clear. It has been suggested that he was not happy with the way things were going on the board of directors, who at times did not seem to be too clear about the way forward, or simply that he had other projects which demanded his attention.

In the light of this there is something of an irony in the events that would follow and although these are what might be called a 'subplot' to the main

Maryport & Carlisle story it might have been the case that George Stephenson could have become involved with it again. When the plans were being formulated to continue the main line from London to Carlisle beyond Lancaster there was considerable debate about the possible route as there did not seem to be a really obvious one. Two major schemes were considered although there were variations in these. The two main proposals involved a line from Lancaster northwards through, or near to, Kendal (and one which the Kendal party fought hard to realise) and from thence on towards Penrith (again, which the party there were keen to see adopted). The other main scheme was a line which would go westwards and round the coast to Carlisle. George Stephenson supported the latter which although it involved crossing Morecambe Bay, would follow a more favourable terrain.

If Stephenson's preference had been successful he might well have found himself dealing with the Maryport & Carlisle again as part of this scheme. In the event it was the route touching the edge of Kendal and on through Penrith which was deemed the more practical one.

1840

With the prospect of the revenue from the transportation of coal being high on the agenda, the first section of the line to be built from Maryport to the coal pits of Arkleby and Oughterside, just over seven miles in length, opened on Wednesday 15th July. At this stage the company owned two locomotives, both built by Tulk & Ley. No. 1 *Ellen* was a 2-2-2 and No. 2 *Brayton* was an 0-6-0. There appears to be no clear evidence relating to how these two locomotives were delivered but Tulk & Ley was based near Whitehaven and so it is reasonable to assume they came by sea to Maryport, given the difficulty of an overland journey. However, at a later stage when a further section of the line was to be opened there was something of a cavalcade when a locomotive from Carlisle was brought in and a crowd gathered to watch.

The opening of this first section appears to have been a fairly low key event, not enhanced by the very inclement weather, and yet in spite of this it is reported large crowds turned out to witness the occasion and all the shops were closed. At about 11.00am the directors and friends took their seats on the train which then set off from Maryport. Presumably by way of emphasising one of the main purposes of the line, when the train reached Oughterside, 20 wagons of coal were attached from the pit and on returning to Maryport these wagons were immediately shipped on board a vessel. A second train brought a further 20 wagons of coal from another of the pits and these were also shipped. There followed a dinner in Maryport which was 'thinly attended'. Fretcheville Lawson Ballantine Dykes on this occasion presided as Chairman. Some speeches were made expressing the view that the line had favourable prospects. During this year the Secretary was William Mitchell. He would hold this office until 1846.

1841

During February there was good news for the company when it was announced that the Gilcrux Colliery would again be conveying its coals using the line for shipment from Maryport. In the light of this move it was confidently expected that at the next half-yearly meeting a four or five per cent dividend would be declared.

In an advert in the *Carlisle Journal* on 10th April the directors stated that they were ready to receive tenders for loans of money in mortgage of their undertaking in sums not less than £100 for three, five or seven years. Interest would be 5 per cent per annum paid half-yearly.

On Monday 12th April a further section of the line was opened, from Arkleby Pit to Aspatria. At just over a mile in length this did not appear to merit any sort of ceremony. It might seem that by way of incentive, on 17th April, the following encouraging statement appeared in the local press:

Maryport and Carlisle Railway
We hear with pleasure that the coal traffic on this railway is already very heavy and as several new pits are fast approaching a state of completion it may be assumed it will yet greatly increase. The passenger traffic is also considerable.

In spite of this it seems there were some problems with William Irving, a contractor. He maintained that there had been at times a lack of progress in getting on with the work because there had been interference by 'officials'. These so-called officials do not seem to have been named and there appears to be no indication as to what sort of interference was involved. However, it must have been significant because a court case ensued. The contractor won the case and was awarded £3,750 which was certainly not an insignificant sum at the time.

1842

At a half-yearly meeting in February it was reported that the work between Wigton and Carlisle was progressing very satisfactorily and there had been an increase in the number of passengers and traffic on the section already opened. There was agreement to petition Parliament in order to divert the line between Aspatria and Wigton, together with a further extension of powers for general purposes, following the recommendations put forward by the Engineer, John Blackmore.

In readiness for the next phase and the first half-yearly meeting, on Friday 5th August, the company placed an advertisement in the press. It was addressed to 'Iron Masters, Founders and others'. Tenders were invited for 800 to 900 tons of malleable iron rails with an average weight of between 60 and 62 lb. per yard. The rails were to be parallel with square ends and with tops and bottoms of the bars similar and each rail 15ft in length. They were to be rolled from the best English refined Iron No. 2 and were to be delivered to the quay at Maryport harbour or at the Carlisle canal basin. Delivery was to be included in the price. Also 'chairs of the best foundry metal to be made by cold blast with joint chairs to be one fifth of the quantity. The whole quantity should be about 302 tons'.

There was also a notice for 'Founders'. This involved the tenders for castings of metal tops for three bridges for roads over the railway; one of 22ft span and a 25ft roadway, one of 22ft 6in. span and 25ft roadway and a third of 32ft span and 25ft roadway. Tenders were to be in by 9th August and among the signatures was that of John Blackmore.

An event which apparently gave rise to local excitement took place on Saturday 2nd July, when a locomotive was brought to the Wigton end of the line. Built by Hawthorn & Co. in Newcastle, it was named *Ballantine Dykes*. The locomotive took its name from the Ballantine Dykes family of Dovenby Hall. It came over from Carlisle on a waggon which was pulled by 11 horses and must have been an impressive sight. Probably, for many people, this was the first opportunity to see one of these remarkable new machines. There were those who came to witness the event and also many who came later to see it once it had been put on the rails. Why *Ballantine Dykes* was brought over at this stage is not made clear and remains speculative. It would be used later with two more of that company's locomotives for the opening ceremony.

It was in this year that J.P. Senhouse stood down as Chairman. Some reports stated that he had resigned but there appears to be no evidence about the circumstances and he continued to have a significant influence in the company. The position passed to F.L.B. Dykes of Dovenby Hall.

1843

In a further step for what had been planned, at the beginning of the year, on Saturday 11th February, and in readiness for the opening of a further and a more substantial section of the railway, another announcement appeared in the press, that there was 'To be let' the building of coaches. Required were two each of first and second class coaches, ten 'trucks' for goods, two close carriages for horses, four for cattle and sheep, two for carriages and light vehicles and in addition metal castings for the bridge at Wigton and 'various minor articles belonging to the above'. The plans and specifications would be lodged at the Office of G. Mounsey. Submissions should be in on, or before, 22nd February and no later than 1pm on the latter. The item was again signed by John Blackmore.

With work on the line from Wigton to Carlisle completed and prior to its opening, an inspection was carried out on behalf of the Board of Trade by General Paisley. So often in this period the inspectors had military connections. He pronounced the line was of a standard that permitted it to be opened and it is said that he was especially impressed by the iron skew bridge over the River Caldew near Cummersdale. So, with the inspector's approval, all was now ready.

On Monday 1st May, the directors took a trip along the section to be opened from Wigton to Carlisle and everything was approved as being in order. It was reported, however, that because of an 'unclear mishap', the locomotive on reaching the station did not stop in time 'and found its way through a temporary shed but without serious injury to the engine or the passengers'.

Wednesday 3rd May was the date set for opening this next section of the railway along a substantial part and giving access to Carlisle. At this stage the railway had a terminus at Bogfield but was able to run into Carlisle on the line of the Newcastle & Carlisle Railway as specified in the Act. Later Bogfield would be abandoned and a change effected.

What a day the opening of this section turned out to be. A horde of people came out to an event the like of which many – indeed probably most – had never experienced before. It clearly eclipsed the first opening. Early in the morning three of the directors, F.L.B. Dykes, J.P. Senhouse and G. Craven, accompanied by others arrived at Wigton to superintend the various arrangements which had been carefully planned. The weather was remarkably fine and this further encouraged great numbers of people from the town and the villages along the line to turn out. Many strangers from different parts of the country were present – Maryport, Aspatria, the Abbey Holme and 'other parts of the west'. At 12.00 noon all the shops closed and the streets by now were crowded. Then there was a general movement towards the temporary station near the windmill (which had been dressed with flags) to the north of the town.

Given that the link to Maryport had yet to be completed, M&CR's locomotives No. 1 *Ellen* and No. 2 *Brayton* were not available, being on the other section of the line. As a result, two of the three locomotives which were to be used for this auspicious occasion – *Star* and *Nelson* – were loaned by the Newcastle & Carlisle Railway and turned up in the early part of the afternoon. It is said 'the whole place seemed full of life and enjoyment'.

By one o'clock the trains had been filled with passengers and it was reported that these included 'many of the fair sex who seemed not the least interested'! In the first carriage of the first train there was a band from Wigton which played the National Anthem (*God save the Queen* in this period with Victoria on the throne) and with those formalities over, at 1.23pm the trains set off keeping at a respectable distance because the object was safety not speed.

The trains passed through Dalston and many of the people who flocked to watch them go past had never seen such a sight before and so what a revelation this must have been. A new age was dawning. The trains eventually ran onto the line of the Newcastle & Carlisle Railway and into the station at London Road. Here again, a great crowd waited to welcome them. It seems this destination was just for this occasion because the company described Bogfield as the terminus of the line, although it was taking steps by way of a Bill to seek alternatives. The trains subsequently returned their passengers to Wigton.

Remarkably, perhaps, after such a splendid event it transpired there were some grumbles. These were to do with the proposed times of trains from Wigton. It was stated that they did not give 'satisfaction' as they would only provide 1½ hours to do business in Carlisle. The directors were asked to take note of this. In addition some were not happy that there were no plans to provide a Sunday service.

After this grand opening, as was usual in this day and age and certainly what was to become very much the custom when railway schemes were completed and opened, there was a grand feast for the directors and their invited guests. It was held in the Kings Arms and started at 5.00pm, going on for four hours. There were numerous speeches with, it would seem, most present wanting to get a word in at some point. The Chairman for the occasion was F.L.B. Dykes, and after the preliminaries of drinking the Queen's health and several other members of the Royal Household, he expressed satisfaction for the day's events and expressed the hope that it was a good omen for the future. He did point to the matter of the recent 'bubbles' affecting some railway projects and the subsequent ruin of the investors who had been caught out in this way but he expressed confidence in their scheme. There had been difficulties with Parliament but the people of Wigton could now travel to 'the capital of the County' in half an hour and to 'the metropolis' in 17 hours. Lime and coal would make Wigton a trading centre and the new road being built would reduce the distance by three miles between the railway and Cockermouth and that would surely bring traffic to the line. In addition, with the line completed with a link to the Newcastle & Carlisle Railway, it would shorten the distance between 'the eastern and western shores'.

There followed a series of speeches, one including thanks to Mr Blackmore for his work as Engineer. He, in turn, thanked Mr Scott the Assistant Engineer for the line. There was much optimism in the air. So, albeit still without a complete line, the Maryport & Carlisle had reached Carlisle. Soon there would be others.

The Newcastle & Carlisle had been the first to get there 13 years previously. Eventually other companies would follow as Carlisle became a focal point of the railway network and this resulted in problems some of which would involve the Maryport & Carlisle.

At this stage the station at Dalston was of a temporary nature. There had been a plan to build the stations along this section in stone 'with appropriate adornments' but this never happened.

For the moment the Maryport & Carlisle and the Newcastle & Carlisle did not see each other in any sense as rivals. Far from it, and because the two could see their eventual way to providing the very important east to west link, they worked side by side without any problems. Initially the former had a terminus with a station at Bogfield, although the company saw this as being an interim situation. They had made plans to establish a more permanent station at Crown Street in their scheme of 1843, but the Bill failed in this element. However, they did have a junction onto the Newcastle & Carlisle which gave access to London Road station. There was some inconvenience for the Maryport & Carlisle trains using this station because it was necessary to reverse in order to enter it.

Certainly, the Maryport & Carlisle appeared keen to move forward with the opening of the railway and to ensure there was as wide a use as possible. In the press on 6th May the following appeared:

ANNO SEXTO & SEPTIMO

VICTORIÆ REGINÆ.

****

Cap. lxx.

An Act for altering and enlarging the Powers of the Act relating to the *Maryport and Carlisle* Railway. [12th *July* 1843.]

WHEREAS by an Act passed in the First Year of the Reign of Her present Majesty, intituled *An Act for making a Railway from the Town and Port of* Maryport *to the Borough of* Carlisle, *to be called the* Maryport and Carlisle *Railway*, certain Persons were incorporated by the Name of "The *Maryport and Carlisle* Railway Company," and were thereby empowered to make and maintain a Railway, with all proper Works and Conveniences connected therewith, commencing at and from the South Quay of the Harbour and Port of *Maryport* in the Township of *Ellenborough* in the Parish of *Dearham* in the County of *Cumberland*, and near to a certain Coal Steath or Shed there situate, then the Property and in the Occupation of *Humphrey Senhouse* Esquire, and passing from thence into and through the several and respective Parishes, Townships, and Places in the said Act mentioned, and terminating by a Junction with the *Newcastle-upon-Tyne and Carlisle* Railway, at, in, or near a certain Field or Close of Land called by the Name of *Bogfield*, in the Township of *Botchergate* in the Parish of *Saint Cuthbert, Carlisle,* in the said County: And whereas the said Company were in and by the said Act empowered to raise amongst themselves any Sum of Money for the Purposes of

7 W. 4. & 1 Vict. c. 101.

[*Local.*]   24 B   the

Expeditious Travelling between Whitehaven and Carlisle in Four Hours
On and after 10 May the Maryport and Carlisle Railway in connection with Messrs Croall, Henderson and Fearon will convey passengers twice daily (Sundays excepted) from Carlisle to Whitehaven and vice-versa,

Going east from	Whitehaven	9.15	3.15
	Maryport	11.00	4.55
	Aspatria	11.30	5.30
	Wigton	12.30	6.30
	Carlisle *arrive*	1.15	7.15
Going west from	Carlisle	9.45	3.45
	Wigton	10.30	4.30
	Aspatria	11.30	5.30
	Maryport	12.00	6.00
Reaching	Whitehaven	1.45	7.45

Fares First Class 2s.   Second Class 1s. 6d.

'The Engineer Coach' in connection with the Railway will leave Whitehaven daily (Sundays excepted) at a quarter past nine in the morning and a quarter past four in the afternoon and The Royal Hotel, Carlisle at half past nine in the morning and half past two in the afternoon.

No extra charge will be made for passengers going to Aspatria, Maryport, Workington or Whitehaven nor will the luggage be removed from the coach till it reaches its destination. Passengers and parcels booked at Aspatria, Maryport, Whitehaven and Workington at The Royal Hotel Coach Office'.

By order of the Directors
William Mitchell, Secretary

For a comparatively small company the Parliamentary procedures come thick and fast as it tried to get its house in order. A further Act, Vict. cap. lxx, was placed on the statute book on 12th July. 'An Act for altering and enlarging the Powers of the Act relating to the Maryport and Carlisle Railway'.

Once again this is a very lengthy document and runs to 18 pages. It has a great deal to do with financial matters and involves the ability to raise further monies. This was to be done by creating more shares with each share to be deemed personal estate. The manner in which shares was to be issued is set out in great detail giving the way in which they were to be bought and the various conditions attached to them. A further element explains the conditions for 'The Purpose of providing of the Railway for the Relief of the Poor be it enacted'.

Section XX describes the approved 'Alterations and Improvements' and these cover the line 'commencing from the Harbour and to terminate by a junction with the Newcastle-upon-Tyne and Carlisle Railway at or near a certain Field or Close of Land called by the name of Bogfield in the town of Botchergate'. The documents and plans are very detailed and in a rather unusual proviso with an Act it makes it clear 'that if help is required by anyone who wishes to examine the documents and plans, copies can be made, the cost to the Clerk of the Peace will be one shilling for every inspection and a shilling for every hour beyond the first hour and sixpence for every hundred words copied'.

ANNO SEPTIMO

VICTORIÆ REGINÆ.

****

Cap. xxxvi.

An Act to amend the Acts relating to the *Maryport and Carlisle* Railway, and for making certain Extensions and Branches connected therewith. [6th *June* 1844.]

WHEREAS an Act was passed in the First Year of the Reign of Her present Majesty Queen *Victoria*, intituled *An Act for making a Railway from the Town and Port of Mary-port to the Borough of Carlisle, to be called " The Maryport and Carlisle Railway:"* And whereas an Act was passed in the Session of Parliament held in the Sixth and Seventh Years of the Reign of Her said present Majesty, intituled *An Act for altering and enlarging the Powers of the Act relating to the* Maryport and Carlisle *Railway:* And whereas it is expedient that Power should be given to make an Extension of the said Railway from its present Terminus as the same is authorized to be made by the said Acts or one of them, commencing at, in, or near a certain Field or Close of Land called or known by the Name of *Bogfield*, belonging to *Eleanor* the Wife of *Henry Dundas McClean* Esquire, and terminating at or near *Crown Street;* also another Extension or Branch Railway commencing at, in, or near the said last-mentioned Field or Close of Land, and terminating in a Field or Close of Land belonging to *John Studholme;*

7 W. 4 & 1 Vict. c. 101.

6 & 7 Vict. c. 70.

[*Local.*]   15 *O*   and

Section XXV emphasises that the company shall not deviate from the line of the plans by more than 100 yards or ten yards in a town or city. The following three lengthy sections give highly detailed conditions regarding the restrictions of the boundaries of the line. Further sections relate to the bridges and deal with any actions that may be brought against the company.

1844

A special meeting was convened on Wednesday 14th February following the usual half-yearly meeting. The directors wanted to make a number of points. The first was that 'they had devoted their entire attention to forcing the line through' and it was anticipated that the whole line would be open before the autumn of that year. William Mitchell, the Engineer, stated out that he was confident it would be done by November. It turned out that he was rather over-optimistic in this prediction. There was good news because Dykes intended to introduce 'extensive lime traffic' once it had been completed and also the newly-opened coal mine at Dearham would soon be providing an estimated £1,500 income per annum. Other sources of income meant that a dividend of 5 per cent was anticipated. The present proposal for a line from Maryport to Whitehaven was welcomed and the prospect of passengers being able to use the Maryport & Carlisle in order to travel further afield going south by using the Lancaster & Carlisle Railway could well bring benefits.

The main part of the business was yet to come. This was the matter of the provision of stations at Carlisle. The view was expressed that the outlook had seemed promising from the company's point of view. The land in Crown Street intended for a station had been purchased, but there had been discussions about having one station in Carlisle for all the companies to use. The directors certainly felt this would be the most convenient solution.

However, because the discussions had become so protracted it was felt the time had come to move forward in getting their own station, with the result that a decision had been made once again to seek Parliamentary approval in the next session to build a station on the land at Crown Street. It was agreed the Bill should go forward.

The outcome was a further Act. This is a comparatively short document, running to just six pages. However, some sections had ramifications which would lead to problems in future years. Vict. cap. xxxvi of 6th June, 1844 relates: 'An Act to amend the Acts relating to the Maryport and Carlisle Railway and for making certain Extensions and Branches connected therewith'. The main purpose of this Act was to give the Maryport & Carlisle the go-ahead to build a station at Crown Street and the part of the Act which must have brought joy to the company was the section which read:

> Power should be given to make an Extension of the said Railway from its present Terminus as the same is authorized to be made by the same Acts or one of them, commencing at, in or near a certain Field or Close of Land called or known by the name of Bogfield, belonging to Eleanor the Wife of Henry Dundas McLean Esquire and terminating at or near Crown Street.

It also allowed the building of 'Works' at the site. There were certain sections in this Act with constraints which gave rise later to problems. One such long statement reads:

> ... provided always that the said first-mentioned Extension of the said Railway shall not be made without the Consent of the *Newcastle-upon-Tyne and Carlisle* Railway Company in Writing under their Common Seal for that Purpose first had and obtained nor without the like consent of the *Lancaster and Carlisle* Railway Company unless the said last-mentioned Company shall obtain Powers from Parliament to make such an Alteration in the line of their Railway as will prevent its coming into contact with the Works of the said *Maryport and Carlisle* Railway Company as authorized by this and the said recited Acts in which case such last-mentioned Consent shall not be necessary.

Sections XII and XIII point to caveats relating first to the Newcastle & Carlisle Railway and, perhaps more significantly, the second of these to the Lancaster & Carlisle Railway.

> Provided also, and be it enacted, That nothing in this Act contained shall extend to prejudice, diminish, alter or take away any of the Rights, Privilege, Powers and Authorities vested in the *Lancaster and Carlisle* Railway Company under an Act passed in the present Session of Parliament but all Rights, Privileges and Franchises of the said Company ... are saved and reserved to the said last-mentioned Company as if this Act had not been passed, so always, nevertheless, that such Rights, Privileges ... be not exercised in such Manner as to prevent the said *Maryport and Carlisle* Railway Company from compulsorily taking and using Land of sufficient Breadth to admit of the Formation of the Extensions and Branches secondly and thirdly herein-before authorized, such Extensions and Branches however, not to exceed respectively Twenty-two Feet in Breadth at the level of the Rails with sufficient Breadth for the necessary Slopes.

This matter would come up again later. The company was required to complete the work within four years. In fact Crown Street station opened in December with the closure of Bogfield. The Maryport & Carlisle would use this station for nearly five years, but there would be issues with the Lancaster & Carlisle Railway as the latter pressed forward to complete its section in the link of the West Coast line from Euston to Scotland. The Lancaster & Carlisle had also been looking to establish a station in Carlisle and problems would arise in its dealing with the Maryport & Carlisle over the issue of that piece of land.

Chapter Two

The line is completed, 1845-1850

1845

On 25th January a notice appeared in the *Carlisle Journal* announcing that there was to be an auction at Wigton on Tuesday 11th February. The contractors, Blackstock & McKay, would be selling cart and waggon horses which had been used on the Wigton to Aspatria contract now that section of the line was completed.

With one of the main objectives in building the Maryport & Carlisle being the opportunity to serve the local collieries the section opened first was the one able to do this. Then followed the second section, also for this purpose, and subsequently the section from Wigton to Carlisle which, in order to meet the requirements of the Act, would be built next.

It was still not possible for passengers to board a train at Maryport and arrive at Carlisle without a break in the journey. On arriving at Aspatria they had to leave the train and board a 'coach' (wagonette) which would take them the eight miles to Wigton where they would travel on a train to complete the journey. Many found this 'Victorian rail replacement service' very inconvenient and for some it was not clear why the company had not made more of an effort to complete the line sooner.

This last segment to be completed was tackled in two sections, one from Aspatria and the other from Wigton to meet at Low Row. On Thursday 30th January the 'missing link' was ready for inspection, carried out by Capt. Coddrington, the government inspector. He informed the company the line could be opened for passengers on Monday 10th February. Brookfield, an interim station, which had been opened on Monday 2nd December the previous year, was closed on this date.

It might have been thought that the significant step of completion would call for a great deal of celebration. However, the directors decided there would be as little ceremony as possible. Nevertheless in this period 'as little ceremony as possible' was a comparative term! The directors met at Maryport to travel the line and there was a very large gathering of local inhabitants, many of whom were decked 'in holiday array' in the fine but rather hazy weather.

The directors' boarded at 10.00am, their train drawn by the 'Dykes' locomotive (presumably this refers to No. 3 *Ballantine Dykes*). The spectators cheered and another train followed closely behind. A minor problem, which slowed down progress, was that the rails were greasy. In spite of this the train managed to reach Aspatria by 10.30am.

There were several trains with cheap fares (3s. 0d. first class, 2s. 0d. second class) running from each end of the line and referred to as 'pleasure trips'. It is reported that 'many hundreds' travelled. The carriages were supplied by Barton & Tweddle and in spite of being overcrowded, were described as 'comfortable'.

It was noted there was still further work needed on the new section from Aspatria to Wigton which included some on the embankments. However, the line enabled the directors' train to travel at 'a rattling pace' wrote one reporter and it reached Crown Street station just before noon.

The second train was delayed by an accident in the boiler of the locomotive and as a result the locomotive *Ellen* had to be called into service. The following comment was included in the report:

> The completion of the line which was constructed considerably beyond the time specified in the Prospectus is highly creditable and those who were determined to throw obstacles in the way of completion have failed to do so!

Whilst there may have been a decision 'to have as little ceremony as possible', again it would seem that such an event could not pass without the directors arranging a 'dinner'. This appeared to be more like a banquet and was held at the Senhouse Arms, starting at 5.00pm. Following the meal the Chairman, Dykes, toasted 'Success to the Maryport and Carlisle Railway' and this was followed by a legion of other toasts and counter toasts with, once again, most of those present appearing to make some sort of a contribution. So, at long last, and somewhat overdue, the line between Maryport and Carlisle was completed.

At the half-yearly meeting held on Wednesday 12th February the directors felt a major milestone had been passed as they expressed 'great satisfaction in having commemorated the entire opening of the railway between Maryport and Carlisle for traffic of every description'. It was made clear that the objective was to develop the system and they were not slow to point out that they, the directors, had faced many difficulties which (they were happy to say) had been overcome. The shareholders were assured that 'prospects were most flattering'.

To back up their optimism it was pointed out that the traffic in coal had reached between 900 and 1,000 wagons to Maryport each week and in addition it was possible to move it forward to Carlisle and beyond. 'Now that Mr Dykes has completed his lime kilns', they were informed, 'transport of it would provide a great source of income for the railway'. Even further there would be connections now between 'the North of Ireland' and the east of England and goods had been coming in from Newcastle and Northumberland. In connection with what was expected in the increase in trade, the harbour at Maryport was being improved and extended. A dividend of 5 per cent was possible.

So the future at this point seemed very rosy. Even so it would not turn out to be the plain sailing they might have hoped for and there would be problems which would start in the following year.

In October it was announced the following timings would be put in place.

	Leaves Maryport		Reaches Carlisle		
	hours	mins.	hours	mins.	
Goods Train	7	30	9	30	Morning
Quick Train	10	15	11	30	Morning
Ditto	4	30	5	45	Evening

THE LINE IS COMPLETED, 1845-1850

	Leaves Carlisle hours mins.		Reaches Maryport hours mins.		
Quick Train	10	35	11	50	Morning
Goods Train	2	0	4	0	Afternoon
Quick Train	6	0	7	30	Evening
Coach leaves Whitehaven	in the Morning at		8	15	
Ditto	in the Afternoon at		2	15	
Coach leaves Maryport	at Noon		12	00	
Ditto	in the Evening		7	30	

1846

The *Carlisle Patriot* for 18th May, 1846 carried this timetable.

Through trains going east

	No. 1 Goods and 1st, 2nd & 3rd class Passengers	No. 2 Quick Train 1st & 2nd class Passengers	No. 3 Goods and 1st & 2nd class Passengers	No. 4 Quick Train 1st & 2nd class Passengers
Leave				
Harrington		8.47am	1.42pm	4.10pm
Workington		9.00	1.55	4.25
Maryport	7.15am	9.20	2.15	4.45
Aspatria	7.50	9.40	2.50	5.05
Wigton	8.25	10.05	3.25	5.30
Carlisle (*arrive*)	9.05	10.35	4.00	6.00

Harrington to Maryport 7.35pm 3rd class passenger train.

Sunday trains going east

	No. 1 1st, 2nd & 3rd class	No. 2 1st, 2nd & 3rd class
Leave		
Harrington	8.00am	4.00pm
Carlisle (*arrive*)	9.48	5.48

Through trains going west

	No. 1 Goods and 1st, 2nd & 3rd Class Passengers	No. 2 Quick Train 1st & 2nd Class Passengers	No. 3 1st & 2nd Class Passengers	No. 4 Quick Train 1st & 2nd Class Passengers
Leave				
Carlisle	7.00am	9.35am	1.30pm	5.35pm
Wigton	7.45	10.05	2.15	6.05
Aspatria	8.20	10.30	2.50	6.30
Maryport	8.50	10.35	3.25	7.00
Workington		11.15	3.45	7.20
Harrington (*arrive*)		11.28	3.53	7.28

Maryport to Harrington 8.00am 3rd class passenger train.

	Sunday trains going west	
	No. 1	No. 2
	1st, 2nd & 3rd class	1st, 2nd & 3rd class
Leave Carlisle	8.00am	4.15pm
Harrington (*arrive*)	9.48	6.03

As the year progressed there developed an issue leading to a disagreement between the Maryport & Carlisle and the Lancaster & Carlisle companies which would eventually reach epic proportions. It involved the plot of land which according to the Lancaster & Carlisle, through their Act, belonged to that company and part of which, it was argued had, in effect, possibly been misappropriated by the Maryport & Carlisle in building the station at Crown Street. There was confusion because it seems the plot would appear to be the same as that apportioned in the Maryport & Carlisle Act.

With no clear way forward the Lancaster & Carlisle decided to take the matter to court and it ended up in the jurisdiction of the Vice-Chancellor. Clearly he found the business rather trying and he stated during the hearing that it appeared to him 'like a game which Indian jugglers played when tossing one ball from one hand to another and it was done so quickly that you could not tell which hand had the ball'. In the end he came down on the side of the plaintiff, namely the Lancaster & Carlisle, because they had made the first contract and so had the right to benefit from the plot of land. In other words it was decided the Maryport & Carlisle would have to relinquish it. This, however, would not be the end of the matter.

It was reported that a large number attended the half-yearly meeting held on Thursday 20th August. Several shareholders took issue with the directors and this was even before dealing with the main business. Reference was made to the repeated comments being reported in the newspapers relating to the alleged mismanagement of the company. The spokesman for the shareholders was G.C. Mounsey. He asked that he might have a list of shareholders in a form which could be easily followed and he maintained that the present list was not in accordance with what was required in law because, in effect, the number of shareholders was not disclosed. A lengthy debate followed about the form the list should take. One issue was that some shareholders' names appeared more than once and this seemed a questionable practice. The directors countered this by saying that this was because certain shareholders had bought at different times. Then came a motion that a list of shareholders in alphabetical order, together with the number of shares each held up to 1st July, should be printed and copies sent to all the shareholders. This was carried.

This, however, was not the end and a very protracted debate followed in which the directors came under some very heavy criticism which further brought out how lax they had been with some aspects of the affairs of the company. The directors tried to counter this by claiming they had been working hard on the improvement of traffic and especially so with that in 'the North of Ireland'. It was said the revenue had been rising with a 16 per cent increase in coal traffic, 34 per cent in passenger traffic and 121 per cent in general goods traffic. They argued the railway was in a prosperous condition. Efforts were being made to complete the double line as far as Aspatria and the greater part was now done. In addition there had been a provisional agreement with the Lancaster & Carlisle Railway for the use of their station at Carlisle. It was felt a shared station would be a benefit for travellers and could ease journeys when having to change trains. The matter of the late running of a considerable number of trains on the line, with 30 minute delays being quite common, was raised. It was hoped this would be rectified once the line was complete and when the work on the double lines had been finished.

The move to the approval of the accounts led to yet another debate with some of the shareholders insisting they could not approve them without having a chance to examine them first. For all this, much had come to light which reflected poor management and following the report of this meeting there was also a damning article in the press. This laid bare in no uncertain terms the perceived shortcomings in which the company had been run. The *Carlisle Journal* reported that:

> *Revolution in the Maryport and Carlisle Railway*
> The day of reckoning has come at last and at length the Directors of the Maryport and Carlisle have opened their eyes to the necessity of a thorough change of the slip-shod mode of conducting the affairs of the line from which the public and the shareholders have so long suffered.

It went on to list the reasons why there had been so much displeasure amongst the shareholders relating to the way the committee had been operating. According to the article, these shortcomings included estimated costs having doubled, estimated revenue not being reached, working expenses having increased by 100 per cent, the value of shares being exaggerated by statements of expected profits which existed only in the imagination, empty promises and fictitious dividends. Even more seriously, a considerable number of shares which remained at the disposal of the committee after the line was operating were sold on the faith of the revenue promised by the Board at a premium as high as £15 per share. From the proceeds of these sales there was made a dividend as if from the working profits of the line. Those who paid the premium were deceived by unfounded estimates of revenue and made to contribute by this deception to the only dividend that the concern was ever in a condition to pay to the other shareholders.

These revelations provoked anger when they came to light and the proprietors called for the dismissal of the Secretary who was held responsible. There was a call for a complete change in 'the system' and for reform. The one positive aspect was the assurance by the Board that with the line improving, 'bona fide' dividends would improve.

In view of all this it was suggested that the capital account should be closed and 'when the real position had been ascertained and mismanagement could no longer hide itself in new expenditure', then by proper management not least in studying the economy it would be possible to recover the ground that had been lost. As if to stress the point further, there followed a letter from 'A subscriber' which served to emphasise the seriousness of the situation.

Following this meeting the directors felt it was necessary to make a statement without delay to the travelling public in relation to the criticisms which had been made about the alleged poor timekeeping of the services it was running and arranged for a piece to be placed on the front page of the *Carlisle Journal* on 29th August. Headed 'To the public', it acknowledged the dissatisfaction that had arisen from the way the company had been managed and went on to point out 'that it is the unanimous wish of the Directors that every possible attention should be paid to the convenience and comfort of every passenger who may travel on this line'. It recognised that all necessary steps should be taken to enable this to happen not only for passengers but also for goods and parcels as well. The public was informed that any complaint concerning the irregularity of the trains should be reported to G.C. Mounsey and T.C. Heysham.

During 1846 William Mitchell stood down as Secretary and was replaced by G.H. Barnes. For some reason the latter held the position for only a short time and was replaced by S.H. Sale who was in office by 1849. He would also not stay for long.

1847

The directors were clearly determined to appease the misgivings of some of the shareholders and at a half-yearly meeting in August made sure copies of the accounts had been circulated beforehand. The news was encouraging and progress was noted. Traffic receipts for the week ending 3rd July showed further steady growth. Passenger returns were £424 0s. 3d. and 'Goods and Cattle' were £276 1s. 9d. This total of £700 2s. 0d. showed an increase of £74 5s. 0d. on the corresponding period in the previous year and the fact that there had been an increase in revenue of £4,745 since the previous December made encouraging news. The dividend would be 1½ per cent and there would be a balance carried forward of £323 18s.

The Engineer, John Harris, informed the meeting that there had been a disadvantage of working trains on the single line because of increasing traffic. He was able to report that the line had been doubled to Aspatria. Locomotives, coaches and 'carrying stock' were 'up to scratch'. An important development was that the locomotive works had been moved to Maryport and preparations were being made for the provision of extra engines as additional mineral traffic was anticipated.

Further propositions had been made to the Newcastle & Carlisle with regard to a possible amalgamation but there had been no response at the time of the meeting. It would seem that at this point the relationship between the directors and shareholders was, for the moment, rather less turbulent. Even so, significant changes were on the way because George Hudson 'The Railway King' was to become involved.

When George Hudson, a draper in York, inherited a large sum of money unexpectedly from a distant relative, he was shrewd enough to realise that one of the best ways to invest it would be in railways. No doubt he felt that with this innovative revolution, there would be a market which would escalate and he would see his investments pay off handsomely. Further, he became engrossed in the whole enterprise and was heavily involved and a force to be reckoned with in terms of financing and driving schemes forward. He saw how small companies, of which there were many at this stage, would be stronger if they worked together and possibly combined. His efforts in certain quarters eventually led to the formation of the Midland Railway, which became a strong and powerful company. Having acquired control of the York & Newcastle Railway he then moved on to annex the Newcastle & Carlisle Railway. In addition he had taken on the Newcastle & Berwick Railway which amalgamated with the York & Newcastle Railway to become the York, Newcastle & Berwick Railway. Hudson felt it would place him in a stronger position to annex the Maryport & Carlisle. This would, as it were, fill the gap between east and west.

By now, in the light of what had been happening, there was evidence that the directors of the Maryport & Carlisle had set it up without a great deal of expertise but it might be argued these were early days and it was, in some ways, what might be referred to in modern parlance as 'a steep learning curve'. Hudson made an approach to the M&CR and the directors presumably felt it could well prove to be an appropriate step forward. Given what had been happening, it probably looked like a sensible way to move, which it might have been, except for the fact that by this stage Hudson was facing difficulties and running into trouble. In other railway quarters, questions were being asked about his methods, not least as far as financial dealings were concerned, as these seemed to leave much to be desired and for which he would soon have to answer. The background to this was the so-called 'Railway Mania'. There was a growing apprehension and potential shareholders had been put off by the events surrounding the dealings of some companies. People were not only becoming wary of investing, but did not always respond to the 'call up' for the shares they had signed for and this left some companies in a parlous state. 'Bubbles' (scams) were also quite prevalent. These involved bogus schemes which were set up and then abandoned with the organisers claiming the scheme was not viable but investors' money had been used up in the preliminary procedures of setting up a railway. At this time there was no really effective process for redress in these circumstances. Certainly there was a lot of growing caution in the market and so perhaps this drew the directors of the Maryport & Carlisle to look favourably on the approaches Hudson was making.

A meeting of the directors and shareholders together with certain other parties was held on Wednesday 22nd September. It was described as a 'Special Meeting' and reporters had been informed that they would not be admitted. (In spite of this, clearly there were persons present on their behalf because a very detailed account of the meeting appeared in the *Carlisle Journal* on 29th September!)

It was held at the Senhouse Arms Hotel in Maryport and the purpose was to receive:

> The Report of the Committee appointed at the previous half-yearly meeting to negotiate with George Hudson (Chairman of the York, Newcastle and Berwick Railway) and

thereupon to assent or dissent from certain provisional terms of management for the leasing, selling, purchasing or otherwise disposing of the Maryport and Carlisle Railway and the working stock, plant and appurtenances to the York, Newcastle and Berwick Railway Company.

There were 80 proprietors present. F.L.B. Dykes was in the Chair.

The first issue raised was why there were no reporters allowed into the meeting. 'How would members unable to attend be able to know what had taken place?' The Chairman simply stated that all reporters had been made known of the decision well in advance. The meeting was informed that following the resolution passed at the previous meeting, 'the Amalgamation Committee had conferred with Mr Hudson and had agreed terms'. The proposal was that 'Mr Hudson would take possession of the Maryport and Carlisle Railway on 1st October next'. There would be a payment of 4 per cent on share capital. The York, Newcastle & Berwick would take on all the liabilities of the company but not exceeding £450,000 with the option of paying off the present shareholders at par when the York, Newcastle & Berwick pay 9 per cent.

Lord Lonsdale proposed that the resolution should be adopted. In his view in the present circumstances he saw no chance of a 9 per cent dividend because short lines were uneconomical and amalgamation provided economies. He felt the present directors had had great difficulties to deal with, but he did concede that they had not been as successful as might have been hoped.

There was a call for an adjournment for possibly a fortnight to consider the proposal, but there were those who felt that looking at the present state of railway property, the terms should be accepted. Some were not happy with Hudson's 4 per cent. After a considerable discussion the motion was agreed by a majority, it was reckoned, of five to one. So Hudson got his way and on 1st October he took over the Maryport & Carlisle, but it would certainly not be plain sailing. He was taking on a company which was experiencing a good deal of disarray at the start of a very troubled period lasting several years.

Hudson himself, also, was far from being in a strong position and already there were pressing issues arising about his financial dealings with various railway companies including the York, Newcastle & Berwick Railway. Yet he was someone who throughout his career had seen himself very much in charge and the decision maker. An incidence of this and the making of decisions without reference to others occurred on 20th October. There was a report in the press referring to 'King Hudson'. Readers were informed that he had made the decision and decreed 'that one booking office shall suffice for the passengers to and from Newcastle and Maryport at Crown Street Station'. The result was that the chief booking clerk, Mr J. Palmer Dalton, who it seems was very popular with the staff, would be moved on to Blaydon. His colleagues presented him with a silver snuff box. The tone of the article seems to suggest that the writer did not hold Hudson in high regard and probably not without some justification, as time would tell.

1848

At a meeting on 5th September it was announced that the directors had entered into an agreement with 'The Carlisle Annan and Liverpool Steam Company'. Yet again, at the same meeting, it was noted out that negotiations involving the 'Joint Station' had failed and it had been agreed to submit the matter to the decision of a jury. The hope was expressed that there would be a speedy and satisfactory solution.

It was reported that the doubling of the line had so far cost £35,115 5s. 11d. and in general terms there had been a significant drop in income, a situation that was the case in many companies in this period. These downturns were attributed to the disturbances on the Continent* and in Ireland† where there had been a large drop in coal traffic. In spite of all this it was seen as vital to complete the doubling of the line.

1849

During March Hudson displayed obstinacy and, it might be argued, arrogance, which would lead to a most unusual event. It was mentioned earlier that the Vice-Chancellor, when dealing with the early stages of the dispute between the Maryport & Carlisle and the Lancaster & Carlisle, had compared the situation to a juggler, and he was not far wrong. The complexity of it and the attitudes of those involved were making it difficult to resolve. In spite of this he had come down on the side of the Lancaster & Carlisle and yet little progress was being made. By this time there were three stations in Carlisle.

First on the scene had been the Newcastle & Carlisle Railway which had a station situated at the eastern end of where London Road came into the city and was aptly named London Road station. There was also the facility of a goods shed on the site. The Maryport & Carlisle came next and initially had a terminus at Bogfield. With a junction onto the Newcastle and Carlisle this company had permitted the Maryport & Carlisle some use of the London Road station as the two companies initially were on good terms. In a Bill in 1843, the Maryport & Carlisle sought powers to build a station at Crown Street, but this first attempt failed to get Parliamentary approval. A further application succeeded in 1844. The outcome was that the Maryport & Carlisle abandoned Bogfield in 1844 having built its own Crown Street station. Again this was appropriately named in connection with the street on which it stood. The Lancaster & Carlisle opened in 1846 and, working in conjunction with the Caledonian Railway, built Citadel station. This was by far the most convenient station for the city centre. The prime objective of these two companies was to establish a route from London to Glasgow. The ideal arrangement would be for all three companies, along with the Caledonian, to use Citadel station.

---

* The 'Revolutions of 1848' also known as the 'Springtime of Nations'. This period remains the most widespread revolutionary wave in European history and involved the Austrian Empire, Danish states, France, German states, Greater Poland, Ireland, Italian states and Romanian principalities.

† The Young Irelander Rebellion, a nationalist rebellion that took place in July 1848.

Problems had arisen partly because with the increased trackwork each company had in this comparatively small area, the Maryport & Carlisle line now passed over the Lancaster & Carlisle three times on the way to Crown Street station. The Lancaster & Carlisle apparently saw a need to remedy this situation, presumably by allowing the Maryport & Carlisle the use of Citadel station. It might then reasonably, as it appears was its due, take control of the Crown Street site with the intended closure of Crown Street station. Following the decision of the Vice-Chancellor and given the previous Acts, the Lancaster & Carlisle had a claim on this land but sought to make a deal with the Maryport & Carlisle whereby the former would, in effect, take over Crown Street station and the Maryport & Carlisle would use Citadel. There were, however, two problems. The first was that the Caledonian Railway, with its interest in Citadel station, could not agree to the terms which had been proposed whereby the Maryport & Carlisle would use Citadel. The second and perhaps more significant, George Hudson, with his usual attitude towards the financial element, felt the amount proposed by the Lancaster & Carlisle in payment to the Maryport & Carlisle for the Crown Street site was far too low and so moved to block the deal.

All this was in spite of the fact that as a result of this lack of agreement, a special jury had then been summoned before the Coroner at the Court House. This meeting had taken place some weeks previously and the hearing had taken two days. The outcome was that it had been decided that much of the land and property upon which Crown Street station stood must be given over to the Lancaster & Carlisle, as was its due, for the figure of £7,171 4s. 3d. to be paid to the Maryport & Carlisle. The Lancaster & Carlisle had subsequently paid this amount into the Bank of England.

In spite of the fact that there had been all this litigation relating to the Crown Street site and, by Act of Parliament, the Lancaster & Carlisle had been empowered to take on Crown Street station, George Hudson continued to object to the terms because in his view the sum determined was still insufficient. (Some sources reported he wanted £100,000.) This had led to still further legal action being taken, and Mr Blenkinsopp, working with the firm of Swift & Co. in Lancaster, for the Lancaster & Carlisle, had applied for immediate possession of the land. However, Mr Heysham, a director of the Maryport & Carlisle, had refused to allow this.

At this point the Lancaster & Carlisle decided that enough was enough and resolved to take Crown Street by force. The company contacted the High Sheriff of the County and as a result the Under-Sheriff joined by Mr Worthing, the Resident Engineer of the Lancaster & Carlisle, and Mr Blenkinsopp went to the station on the morning of Saturday 17th March. He spoke with the clerks at the station who were the only people present and then crossed the platform and onto the line and announced a formal possession of the site to Mr Blenkinsopp.

The event which followed was by any measure quite remarkable and the like of which may well be without parallel. In reporting it, the local press started the description of the incident with the words: 'The Crown Street Station ground of the Maryport and Carlisle Company was the theatre of a novel and animated scene.'

After Blenkinsopp's announcement, a member of staff of the Lancaster & Carlisle 'waved a handkerchief' and about 150 men appeared with crow bars, pickaxes, spades and similar devices and proceeded to tear up the platforms and pull up the tracks. They then tore down the sheds for the coal and lime depots. It seems all this took only a matter of a few minutes. They then told the staff of the Maryport & Carlisle to take away any items such as documents they wished to retain and, when this had been done, they gutted the station house and took down the whole building.

Mr Bibby, the superintendent of railway police for the Lancaster & Carlisle, and a body of his men took charge of all the entrances to the Maryport & Carlisle station ground and prevented 'uninterested and unauthorised' persons from entering. A man was posted near to where the Maryport & Carlisle line joined that of the Newcastle & Carlisle at about 200 yards distant to inform the driver of the train due in at 11.00am that he could not proceed to the old station. As a result, the train was diverted to the Newcastle & Carlisle station.

Bills were then put up around the town stating that the Lancaster & Carlisle had taken possession of the Maryport & Carlisle station and until further notice trains of that company would start at the Newcastle & Carlisle station. The comment was made in the press that the scene during the demolition was a very animated one and many spectators had turned up to watch what was happening. No resistance was offered.

In order not to inconvenience the public, the Lancaster & Carlisle offered the Maryport & Carlisle temporary use of Citadel station and made preparations for that to happen. The offer was turned down! The Maryport & Carlisle opted for the use of the London Road station.

It was almost inevitable that there would be a considerable amount of local reaction to this incident. It was deprecated by many and there was a view expressed that it was highly desirable that the four companies should act together and unite in the use of Citadel station which was described as 'a splendid and ornamental building and at a cost of £100,000 had space for all'.

Perhaps, inevitably, some laid the blame squarely on George Hudson. It was said that before the Maryport & Carlisle had come under his control it had reached a preliminary agreement with the Lancaster & Carlisle for the use of Citadel Station, but this had also been thwarted by the Caledonian Railway directors who thought the sum stipulated for its use was deemed insufficient.

After this debacle it was hoped that George Hudson would make the effort to construct another station, the entrance to which would be by Crown Street, but this was wishful thinking. It was felt the only satisfactory solution was that Citadel should be shared by the four companies because passengers travelling on the Maryport & Carlisle and the Newcastle & Carlisle arrived at a mile from the centre of the town whereas Citadel station was in the centre. It was also remarked that 'We can assure Mr Hudson that the people of Carlisle will take their interest and convenience into account'.

Before very long 'Mr Hudson' would not be in a position to do so. During 1849 he was faced with a number of allegations of the mishandling of the finances of a considerable number of railway companies including the York, Berwick & Carlisle Railway. Court proceedings were in the offing and eventually Hudson was found guilty on a number of serious charges relating to financial matters. The outcome was that his time with the Maryport & Carlisle would come to an end and he would eventually decide to move (some have said 'flee') to France to try and avoid recrimination from a number of quarters. Meanwhile the Maryport & Carlisle would revert to being controlled by its original owners.

This was not the easiest of times! They would be faced with challenges and if these were to be overcome and the railway was going to survive, face them they must. The aftermath of what had happened led to a special meeting held on Tuesday 16th October. The purpose was to consider what steps should be taken with the York, Newcastle & Berwick Railway and whether there should be a move to lease the line to that company. There was some hesitancy about this. Chairman Dykes explained that the meeting was 'for the purpose of considering what steps should be taken with regard to the possible lease to the York, Newcastle and Berwick Company'.

He went on to remind the meeting that at the last half-yearly meeting in consequence of the confused state of the York, Newcastle & Berwick together with the rejection by the House of Commons of a Bill carrying into the effect the agreement with Mr Hudson on the part of the company the position of the Maryport & Carlisle regarding the leasing of the line was one of considerable uncertainty. There was also the prospect that the Board of the York, Newcastle & Berwick 'could be considerably altered' at its next meeting following the report of a Committee of Investigation. It was decided no further action was advisable and the meeting was adjourned.

Once again the Maryport & Carlisle would retain its independence.

1850

This was to be a very turbulent year and at some point during the course of it S.H. Sale gave up the post of Secretary and Henry Jacob took on the position. In addition to that office he also became the General Manager and this combining of the two roles became a permanent arrangement thereafter.

With these decisions made, on Tuesday 1st January, with George Hudson no longer attached to the company, and no lease in place, the former directors resumed the management of it. They would have quite a struggle pulling things together again and there would be some situations which would lead to a difficult time for the company and for the directors in particular.

On Tuesday 12th February there was growing uneasiness expressed at the half-yearly meeting. Once again misgivings were expressed and this involved the matter of accounting. Exchanges became quite heated when a shareholder took the directors to task for not having the accounts properly audited and doing the auditing themselves. It was claimed the directors were acting illegally and evidence was produced using documentation which appeared to bear this out. The directors clearly saw this as a personal affront and being in a majority at the meeting were in a position to overrule any move to make changes. The worrying feature for some was that the amounts dealt with were considerable, being of the order of £100,000. This uneasiness with the manner in which the Board was acting, would grow.

At a meeting on Wednesday 6th March there was, according to reports, a 'numerous attendance' relating to the results of the negotiations with Hudson following the restoration of their line and the payment of rent due from him to the company for the lease of the line during the 15 months he had held it. The news was brief and not good. The directors had to admit they had nothing to tell the shareholders because they had not received a balance from Mr Hudson. They acknowledged that it was a considerable sum and they hoped to have a settlement shortly. There was also the matter of Crown Street station with the hope of a resolution 'in a short time'. The directors expressed 'a sanguine hope of progress for the line with regard to traffic'.

It then transpired that two of the directors, Messrs Steel and Cowan had managed to meet Hudson and he had told them he had no money and they should call again 'when Allport was present'.* This they had done and presented Hudson with an account by which he was indebted to the company £5,106 5s. 4d.

Hudson had agreed the amount but said he could not pay until April because, again he emphasised, he had no money. He agreed to meet them again in April and added that he had some counter-claims against the company. Perhaps, in typical Hudson fashion, the two of them were then 'bowed out'. (Perhaps knowingly, this comment caused laughter at the meeting.)

The result was there would be no dividend declared at the meeting. The mood changed and the shareholders reacted in anger to this, asking 'Are we being made April Fools?' By way of some sort of sop they were told that if Hudson had paid up, the dividend would have been 4¾ per cent. On receiving this information there was a general consent to wait until April. At this point in time Hudson was in trouble again. Soon he would be brought to reckon for his dubious financial dealing and methods.

By June it was reported that various matters of importance had been given consideration. The first was that the company, having been deprived of the use of Crown Street station, felt this was a great loss because it had caused a good deal of inconvenience. However, the hope was expressed it might be possible to create another station nearby as there was plenty of land available and it was thought it would not prove to be expensive. In the meantime they would try to use the 'General Station'.

It was also admitted out that during the short period when Mr Hudson had possession of their railway most of the materials handed over to him had been 'consumed' and also appropriated to the working department of the railway without being replaced and consequently much expense had been incurred in reinstating this part of the company's stock. The directors did express the hope that they could recover these costs from Hudson and also compensation for the dilapidation to the company's rolling stock. There was also the matter of rent which Hudson owed the company. They said that they had made repeated and urgent applications to him for payments and arbitration was agreed which it was hoped would protect payment.

---

* James Allport who was once described as having grown up with the 'Hudson Gang' and who had an almost pathological love of inter-company quarrelling. At various times he held high office in the Midland Railway.

In September at the half-yearly meeting, which was 'numerously attended' the shareholders were keen to hear the reports from the directors and the auditors. The company now had as Secretary, Mr Jacob. What the gathered community was keen to have was 'a proper understanding between the shareholders and Directors now that we resume the working of the line again upon our own accounts and that there shall be an inquiry into the affairs of the Company in order to satisfy everyone on the subject'.

The Secretary stated that the directors were working for this to happen and might have proposed the plan themselves and that a resolution would be proposed commending an investigation be made. The resolution was simply a proposal in general terms for the purpose of making an enquiry into the state of the company and to report the results to a general meeting. Initially it was agreed that George Harrison, George Saul, William Cowan and G.S. Mounsey should carry out this undertaking and be given full powers to call before them and examine all persons concerned, together with all books, papers and other documents. Clearly this was being taken very seriously.

It was proposed that the meeting should be adjourned until 23rd October for the purpose of receiving the report of the committee. However, before the matter could be concluded it was complained that Harrison was on the committee but as he was a director and given the nature of the inquiry, this was inappropriate. The whole issue was opened up again with the matter of whether there should be any directors on the committee. A lengthy debate followed which included the matter of Harrison's role. The outcome was that Harrison decided to withdraw from the committee and was replaced by G.W. Hartley. There would be other changes later. Again there is something of an indication in all this of a group left struggling after the departure of Hudson and as they tried to move the company along again.

On Saturday 16th November a report became public following the work of the committee set up to look into the company's affairs. It began by restating the purpose of the enquiry, listing those who had undertaken the task; namely G.W. Hartley, George Saul, William Cowan, William Ostle and George Mounsey. They reported that they had asked Quilter, Bell & Co. accountants in London to advise them, needing skills beyond those of the members of the committee.

The report initially notes the original purpose for which the railway was planned and built. It then goes on to state that in the findings of the committee the financial history shows unsound policies to have been pursued to 'ill effect'. This, it is advised, should be a warning for the future. In the view of the committee, there had been concealment which was 'mischievous and also dishonourable to all parties'. There follows detail and this includes the improper manner with which the directors dealt with matters relating to shares and the way in which this had led to a lack of funds. There had also been money borrowed without legal authority. At one point it is noted with surprise that this should not have happened given one of the directors was a solicitor. There is also reference to the fact that appointments were made without proper regard for the salary levels, and also that some of the roles were not clearly defined. The borrowing which continued meant that by the end of 1842 a further sum of

£150,000 was needed to complete the line. This resulted in an Act to raise more capital by issuing more shares and to effect the order from Parliament, certain directors entered into a subscription contract in March 1843. It was said £9,000 had been paid into the bank as a deposit, but there was no evidence this ever happened. Further it had been discovered there were irregularities relating to these shares.

From what had been found by the committee it is clear that the directors had not been acting in the best possible interests of the company although it is not clear what the motives were or, indeed, whether in some instances they were acting in ignorance through lack of knowledge or experience. However, before the meeting was held some were making their views very clear with attacks being made on certain members of the committee and not least about their intentions. A statement made and simply signed by 'A Proprietor' writing on 11th November and published in the press goes into great length in berating the members of the investigation committee, accusing them of misleading the shareholders and that the members of the committee were seeking to control the company.

Strong feelings being expressed on both sides. The language of the writer is particularly harsh. Much of the argument goes back to the manner in which shares were issued and the apparent misuse and misinterpretation involved. 'Remember the interests of the Railway are not promoted by tearing its machinery to pieces'. Again there is the view that the purpose of the members of the 'Investigation Committee' is to throw out the 'old Directors' and get absolute power in doing so. The Chairman of the enquiry committee is particularly singled out for criticism. 'Mr Mounsey is Chairman of the Committee and knows well how to play a deep game. He is at once in pursuit of power and private interest'.

On Wednesday 20th November there was an 'Extraordinary Meeting' attended by the shareholders with the purpose of taking into account what was described as 'the very voluminous and somewhat curious report of the Committee of Investigators' which by now had been circulated among the proprietors. A 'very stormy' discussion was anticipated. It was reported that the meeting was very well attended and that a long and angry discussion ensued which lasted several hours.

However, also in November, in spite of these events, the company announced that it would be submitting a lengthy Bill for Parliamentary consideration. It was headed: 'Deviation and Abandonment of the line, increase of capital, lease of the undertaking and for other purposes'. The Bill outlined the various requirements. It included an application which would be made 'in the ensuing session for leave to bring in a Bill for an Act to alter, amend, extend and enlarge and so far as is necessary to repeal some of the provisions of the several Acts following or some of them'.

The first involved the Act passed,

> ... in the first year of the reign of Her Majesty Queen Victoria being an Act for making a railway from the Town and Port of Maryport to the Borough of Carlisle to be called the Maryport and Carlisle Railway'. Also an Act in the sixth and seventh year of the reign of her Majesty 'for altering and enlarging certain extensions and branches.

The purpose of this action was a proposal to seek powers to purchase by compulsory powers or otherwise a piece of land near the South Quay and Dock Quay at Maryport harbour. This would then involve a scheme to enlarge the station and terminal at the harbour in order to provide additional facilities for the delivery of 'minerals, goods and passengers' from the railway to the docks.

There is a further element by which an extension would be made starting 'at a close of land' referred to as 'Bogfield which is the terminus described in the plans of 1843'. The line would be extended and would link by way of a junction with the Lancaster & Carlisle Railway at a point where the latter crossed Crown Street. A further application would be made to enable the Maryport & Carlisle to 'demise or lease' onto the Newcastle & Carlisle or the York, Newcastle & Berwick or the Lancaster & Carlisle Railway. However, the year would not end without another very turbulent series of events which brought further keen criticism on the way the railway was being run.

The pages of the *Carlisle Patriot* would become something of a battleground with a considerable amount of ink being spent on argument and counter-argument regarding many aspects of the company's procedures and those involved with them in relation to the investigation which had been carried out. The first round of this particular episode appeared on the last page of the *Carlisle Patriot* of 14th December. It is a truly remarkable item taking up about two-thirds of the page and is very detailed. Again, the contributor signs it 'A Shareholder' and it is addressed to other shareholders. Clearly the owner of the newspaper, no doubt together with the editor, felt that the article, in spite of the anonymity, should be made public.

The opening paragraph explains the purpose of writing the account. The report of the Committee of Investigation 'was not circulated among you [the shareholders] till Saturday 16th November leaving two clear days only for you to examine the report and for the Directors to refute the charges of mismanagement brought forward by the Committee against them collectively and individually'. The writer carries out a most detailed analysis from a particular point of view. There is plenty of criticism of a number of individuals and each element of the railway's operations is carefully detailed and to some extent analysed. The headings used are 'General Management, Traffic, Mineral Traffic, Lime, Eastern Coal, Timber, Passengers, Permanent Way, Land and Stations'. This article clearly made an impact because the following week there was a response of a similar length which attempted to address the issues raised the previous week and counter them.

Perhaps the remarkable aspect was that this was no longer just an exchange in meetings but was brought into the public domain. One source described it as 'open warfare'! Further the impact of all this disputation was not being confined just to the local press.

On 21st December, the *Railway Record*, a vital purveyor of information to those with an interest in railway matters not least from the point of view of both investing and checking investments, carried a very lengthy report and in doing so quoted the *Carlisle Patriot* in describing what had been happening in Maryport. This article refers to 'a vast quantity of petty deals' and concludes

'How much therefore it is to be lamented that all these useless criminations and recriminations should have been laid before the public'.

That was not the end. Towards the end of December a swingeing report about the railway appeared in the highly-respected *Herepath's Journal*. It went further than just commenting on the affairs of the Maryport & Carlisle. It accused the company of bringing disgrace on the whole industry. The language is extremely powerful and the writer spares no efforts in expressing very strong views. *Herepath's Journal* reported that,

> The days of the exposure of railway misdoings are not yet over. Far from it. The Investigation Report on the Maryport and Carlisle thrust us again into the thick of them. It would appear that a worse state of things was never brought to light than this report has revealed to the public; it smears to some extent the fair reputations of the rest of the railway world. Justice must be done. [It goes on to highlight] ... mishandling of money, especially in relation to shares, problems arising from Directors forming the majority of meetings and sometimes being the only ones present, shareholders 'not caring a rap' about what is happening and yet now they turn round and complain, the Directors proceeded as though Acts of Parliament were waste paper and were ignored.

There is then an analysis of the handling of the finances, including the way in which money was paid out for dividends when in fact there was no surplus for dividends. 'These matters clearly must be addressed'. The reputation of the Maryport & Carlisle was at rock bottom.

Almost in spite of all this, there was an element of 'business as usual'. It had been announced on the 9th December that the company was 'prepared' to issue season tickets to and from each station on the line and those interested in taking advantage of this and who wanted to know the rates, were advised to make an application to Henry Jacob, the Secretary. Together with all this, the company started a significant overhaul of the fares system.

In this year a further change of company Chairman took place and G.W. Hartley took on the role.

Chapter Three

Pulling together, 1851-1860

1851

The time had come to attempt to bring about a more positive image and the year would see some significant moves being made with the intention of providing better services and facilities. On Monday 19th May the following announcement was placed in the press:

MARYPORT AND CARLISLE RAILWAY
Citadel Station
Notice is hereby given that the PASSENGER TRAINS of this Company will ARRIVE at and DEPART from the CITADEL STATION CARLISLE on and after SUNDAY the 1st of June 1851. Times of Arrival and Departure and other information will be duly made known on the completion of the Company's arrangements

This was signed by Henry Jacob, the Secretary, and would be ratified in an Act issued on 3rd July.

On 7th June a substantial notice was placed on the front page of the *Carlisle Patriot* giving details of the arrangement of services in connection with the Whitsun Hirings and also of a new fare structure which included season tickets.

CHEAP TRAINS FOR THE WHITSUNTIDE HIRINGS
Return Tickets at One Fare and a Half will be issued to First and Second Class Passengers from all Stations
To Maryport on Friday 6th and 7th of June
To Carlisle on Saturday 7th and 13th June
To Wigton on Tuesday 10th June

SPECIAL TRAINS WILL BE RUN
To Carlisle on Saturday 7th June 7h 30m a.m. from Wigton
From Carlisle on Saturday 7th June at 5h and 7.30 p.m. to Wigton
To Wigton on Tuesday 10th June at 8h a.m. from Carlisle
Third Class carriages will be attached to each Special Train

IMPORTANT ALTERATIONS and REDUCTION IN FARES
RETURN TICKETS AVAILABLE FOR THE DAY ONLY ON WEEKDAYS
Return Tickets to 1st and 2nd Class Passengers at
One-and-a-Half Fare to and from all Stations
On Sundays
Return Tickets to 1st 2nd and 3rd Class Passengers at one fare to and from all Stations.

LEAVE CARLISLE ON WEEK DAYS

At 7 0	Morning	1st, 2nd and Parliamentary Class
10 00	"	1st and 2nd
2 35	Afternoon	1st and 2nd
6 30	Evening	1st, 2nd and 3rd Class

ON SUNDAYS

At 8 30	Morning	1st, 2nd & Parliamentary Class
6 0	Evening	1st, 2nd and 3rd Class

LEAVE MARYPORT ON WEEK DAYS

At 7 40	Morning	1st, 2nd & Parliamentary Class
11 10	''	1st and 2nd
3 8	Afternoon	1st and 2nd, Express Mail
7 10	Evening	1st, 2nd and 3rd Class

ON SUNDAYS

At 9 20	Morning	1st, 2nd & Parliamentary Class
6 40	Evening	1st, 2nd and 3rd Class

MARYPORT MARKET DAY

A Third Class Carriage will on Fridays be attached to the train leaving Maryport at 3 08 Afternoon, as far as Aspatria, setting down Passengers at Dearham,* Bullgill,† Arkleby and Aspatria.

There followed a detailed list of these reduced fares from Carlisle to each of the ten stations up to and including Maryport for first, second and third class passengers ranging from, first class 1s. 0d., second class 8d. and third class 6d. to Dalston and to Maryport first class 5s. 2d., second class 3s. 10d. and third class 2s. 11d., then a list of the prices from all the stations from Maryport to Carlisle. The table for trains from Carlisle is:

	1st		2nd		3rd	
	s.	d.	s.	d.	s.	d.
Carlisle to Dalston and vice-versa	1	00	0	8	0	6
Curthwaite	1	5	1	1	0	9
Wigton	2	3	1	8	1	3
Leegate	2	10	2	2	1	7
Brayton	3	4	2	6	1	11
Aspatria	3	8	2	9	2	1
Arkleby	3	10	2	10	2	3
Bullgill†	4	5	3	3	2	6
Dearham*	4	9	3	6	2	8
Maryport	5	2	3	10	2	11

Parliamentary 1 Penny per mile.
With a similar pattern for trains from Maryport.

Finally there was a section about season tickets. 'To accommodate Parties having a Country Residence or desiring Sea Bathing the following liberal Rates for Season Tickets have been adopted'. Once again there was a detailed chart giving the cost of these tickets for first and second class. Presumably it was assumed that those who would normally travel third class were not thought to be the sort who would have country residences or wish to take the train to go

---

* Dearham was renamed Dearham Bridge from 1st June, 1867. With the opening of the Derwent branch, a new station, between Bullgill and Linefoot, took the name Dearham.
† Bullgill is sometimes shown in contemporary documents as two words.

ANNO DECIMO QUARTO & DECIMO QUINTO

VICTORIÆ REGINÆ.

****

Cap. lxxii.

An Act for enabling the *Maryport and Carlisle* Railway Company to make a Deviation in their Line of Railway, and increase their Capital; and for other Purposes. [3d *July* 1851.]

WHEREAS an Act was passed in the First Year of the Reign of Her present Majesty Queen *Victoria*, intituled *An Act for making a Railway from the Town and Port of Maryport to the Borough of Carlisle, to be called "The* Maryport and Carlisle *Railway:"* And whereas another Act was passed in the Session of Parliament holden in the Sixth and Seventh Years of the Reign of Her said present Majesty, intituled *An Act for altering and enlarging the Powers of the Act relating to the* Maryport and Carlisle *Railway:* And whereas another Act was passed in the Seventh Year of the Reign of Her said present Majesty, intituled *An Act to amend the Acts relating to the* Maryport and Carlisle *Railway, and for making certain Extensions and Branches connected therewith:* And whereas it is expedient that the said Company should be enabled to relinquish the Construction of their present authorized Branch between *Bogfield* and *Crown Street* in the Borough of *Carlisle*, and to substitute therefor another Branch, so as to complete their Access to the general Railway Station in the said Borough called the *Citadel* Station, and to enable them to use the same, and to obtain certain Accommodation therein for their Traffic: And whereas by the said first-recited Act

7 W. 4. & 1 Vict. c. 101.

6 & 7 Vict. c. 70.

7 & 8 Vict. c. 36.

[*Local.*]   12 K   the

sea bathing! The piece continued, 'The tickets can be purchased for 12 Month, 6 Month or 3 Month periods'. A first class ticket for three months from Carlisle to Maryport would be £10 0s. 0d. with a second class ticket being £8 15s. 0d. Tickets for a 12 month period would be £21 0s. 0d. and £17 0s. 0d. respectively.

This would be the last year Arkleby would appear on the timetable as it was closed on 1st January, 1852.

Following a further petition to Parliament the Act, Vict. cap. lxxii, was placed on the statute book on 3rd July. It is described as:

> An Act for enabling the *Maryport and Carlisle* Railway Company to make a Deviation in their Line of Railway, to increase their Capital; and for other Purposes.

It goes on to seek approval,

> ... to relinquish the Construction of the present authorized Branch between *Bogfield* and *Crown Street* in the *Borough of Carlisle*, and to substitute therefor another Branch, so as to complete Access to the general Railway Station in the said Borough called the *Citadel* Station, and to enable them to use the same, and to obtain certain Accommodation therein for their Traffic.

The Act further states that approval has been given for,

> ... a branch railway commencing by a Junction at the present authorized line at or near the original terminus of the line in or near a field or close of land by the name of Bogfield in the township of Bogtchergate [sic] and terminating by a junction with the Lancaster and Carlisle at or near the point where the Maryport and Carlisle crosses Crown Street.

It states that the Maryport & Carlisle must abandon the construction in the original plan.

The conditions include a clause which states that the work must be completed within four years. There are also matters relating to finance which include raising no more than £91,000 by way of shares for the work. A further amount could be raised to pay off loans which the company might take. The Act also deals with matters relating to directors of the company and the reduction to 12 with three being needed for a quorum. There is a caveat about respecting the property of the Lancaster & Carlisle Railway and the Caledonian Railway and reference is made to the agreement of 2nd April, which is for 999 years.

There is a section involving the Newcastle & Carlisle and the paying of tolls to the Maryport & Carlisle to use its line in getting to Citadel station. However, because the proposed branch railway of the Maryport & Carlisle would cross the Newcastle & Carlisle, in order to prevent accidents, the Maryport & Carlisle must meet the cost of 'a signal post or signal posts' and also 'keep a competent person' to oversee this situation. Failure to do so would incur a £20 fine and a daily penalty thereafter of £10.

Time would tell that many of these proposals were not actioned just as earlier ones which failed to be acted upon. In some cases it was simply that the time allocated lapsed and four years on it was seen that a complete reappraisal of where the company stood was needed. This would come about in an Act placed on the statute book four years later.

ANNO DECIMO OCTAVO & DECIMO NONO

VICTORIÆ REGINÆ.

****

Cap. lxxix.

An Act to consolidate and amend the Acts relating to the *Maryport and Carlisle* Railway; to authorize the Company to improve their existing Railway; to make new Branches, Stations, and other Additions to their Works; to raise further Moneys; and for other Purposes.

[26th *June* 1855.]

WHEREAS by an Act (Local and Personal) passed in the First Year of the Reign of Her Majesty Queen *Victoria*, Chapter One hundred and one, herein-after called "the Act of 1837," the *Maryport and Carlisle* Railway Company were incorporated for the Purpose of making a Railway from the Town and Port of *Maryport* to the Borough of *Carlisle* in the County of *Cumberland*, there to join the *Newcastle-upon-Tyne and Carlisle* Railway; the Preamble of that Act reciting that such a Railway "would be " productive of great Advantages to the agricultural, manufacturing, " mining, and commercial Interests of the said County and the adjoin- " ing County of *Northumberland*, and to the Public in general, by " affording great additional Facilities for the Transit of Passengers,

1 Vict. c. ci.

[*Local.*]   12 *L*   " Merchandise,

On 26th December an announcement was made that after 1st January, 1852 the goods business of the railway would be removed from the London Road station of the Newcastle & Carlisle to the Bog station of the company. Further it was announced that Arkleby station would close and the business of that station would be transferred to Aspatria.

1852

Arkleby station closed on 1st January.

There was a half-yearly meeting on Tuesday 24th February at the Senhouse Arms in Maryport and in the main the tenor of it was amiable. The acting Chairman, Vice-Chairman G. Harrison, seemed able to cultivate a placid atmosphere during the proceedings and although there were some issues, these were aired without animosity. During the course of the meeting it was reported that although Citadel station had been in use for 'some time' (in fact almost a year) it had taken several months to fix what the rent would be. This had now been done. What was perhaps more encouraging was that it could be stated that any disputes with the Lancaster & Carlisle were at an end and there were plaudits for the way those with whom they had dealt were 'exceedingly liberal, reasonable and straightforward' during the negotiations. How things had changed for the better!

It was also reported that the company was now 'on the most friendly terms with the Newcastle Company' not least because of 'their mutual interest'. What a relief this must have been after all the altercations in the past. The numbers showed that whilst mineral traffic had fallen off, goods and passenger traffic had increased. Mr Tosh was praised for his work on having reduced expenditure in the locomotive department. The matter of developing the harbour at Maryport at a cost of £100,000 was not seen to be something the company was in a position to approve because it appeared this cost would be met by the Harbour Trustees. The terms for the telegraph system had been agreed and this would be run by the Telegraph Company. The accounts were approved after some debate and the dividend set at 4 per cent.

1855

Within four years of the previous Act, and having laid another Bill before Parliament, a further Act was placed on the statute book. The Act, Vict. cap. lxxix, dated 26th June, 1855 stated it was,

> An Act to consolidate and amend the Acts relating to the *Maryport and Carlisle* Railway; to authorize the Company to improve their existing Railway; to make new Branches, Stations, and other Additions to their Works; to raise further Moneys; and for other Purposes.

The preamble in this Act is very lengthy and itemises certain of the objectives in the Acts of 1837, 1843 and 1844. In this Act the purpose initially was to be something of what might be called 'a tidying up process' given a situation that had got rather out of hand in relation to what had been and what had not been done as far as the previous Acts were concerned.

The Act goes on to state,

> And whereas it is expedient that some of the provisions of the recited Acts should be amended and that in order to avoid inconvenience arising from several Acts relating to the same purposes being in force at the same time, the recited Acts (1837, 1843 and 1844) should be repealed and that the Provisions thereof modified and amended, should be consolidated into one Act.

In order to make this effective it was decided that the best way forward was to dissolve the company and then start again.

This may seem a drastic step to take, but given the state that the company was in, and that there is much in the Act about the financial aspects of the whole business, this was seen as the most expedient way forward. The Act states that the new company 'shall be incorporated by the name 'The Maryport and Carlisle Railway Company'. (No surprises there). In the following 24 pages details are set out relating to, a large extent, the organisation of the financial elements and the various schemes already contained in the previous Acts which would be carried forward.

Almost from the outset, railway companies quickly discovered that apart from general traffic there was also revenue to be made by running 'excursions' and 'trips'. People were given the opportunity to visit places which, for most, had been beyond reach and the railways were able to give them freedom to travel further afield than previously. In this period, in many parts of the country it was the agricultural shows which attracted a lot of interest. Along with other companies the Maryport & Carlisle met this need. The Royal Agricultural Society meeting at Carlisle in July of this year was a great attraction and the railway made sure it could provide the means which would enable people to visit it easily by using the train.

An example is an event which took place on Wednesday 25th, Thursday 26th and Friday 27th July. The services provided a wide variety of facilities.

From Maryport	Wednesday, Thursday and Friday
	1st and 2nd Class coaches departing at 9.15 am
	Thursday
	1st, 2nd and 3rd Classes departing at 7.00 am
	Friday
	3rd Class only at 7.00 am
From Wigton for Carlisle	Thursday and Friday
	2nd and 3rd classes only

A train will leave Carlisle at 5.15 pm on the above days.
Also on Thursday and Friday at 9.00 pm for Maryport
On Friday a train will leave Carlisle at 10.15 pm for Wigton enabling parties to view the fireworks.
Regular trains will run as usual.
Tickets at the usual return fares.

On Friday 27th 3rd Class return tickets at one fare will be issued from all stations to Carlisle by the train leaving Maryport at 7.00 am, 8.00 am and Wigton at 7.30 am and returning from Carlisle at 5.15 pm, 9.00 pm and 10.15 pm to Wigton
All trains will stop at all stations.

Joseph Lyndall, Secretary

It will be seen from the signing of these notices by Joseph Lyndall that during the year he had taken over the position recently held by Henry Jacob.

A half-yearly meeting was held on Saturday 8th September at the Court House in Maryport. On the same day, not far away, the ceremony of the cutting of the first sod of the Silloth Railway was taking place. This would be referred to at the meeting, not so much the ceremony but rather the expenditure which the Maryport & Carlisle had paid when fighting in Parliament to try and prevent approval for the Act enabling it to be built. In the first attempt the Silloth scheme had been turned down, but a second submission had proved successful and been approved.

The Maryport & Carlisle was facing some further 'ups and downs' which were reported at the meeting. Although since the meeting in 1854, first and second class passenger numbers were up, those for third class were down. In total, passenger numbers had dropped by over 5,000.

As far as general goods were concerned the parcels traffic was up, the figure for horses and carriages was down and the transportation of coal, lime and other minerals was slightly up, although it was noted that coal traffic was down. There had been necessary expenditure on heavy repairs to the wheels and axles of the coal wagons.

They then returned to a discussion about the company's stance as far as the proposed Silloth Railway project was concerned. It was felt that even though they had lost their case against the Act it had been worth the effort to oppose it, although when it had reached the final stages it was agreed there was no point in further expenditure being used to do so.

Mr Tosh reported that the locomotives which had been purchased between 10 and 14 years ago had, with the exception of No. 5, been rebuilt or replaced by others which had much greater power. He further pointed out that the cast wheels on the coal wagons had been replaced by new malleable ones.

There was some concern expressed about the high rise in the cost of coke which had gone from 14s. 6d. per ton to 20s. 6d. per ton. When everything had been taken into consideration it might have been possible to propose a 4 per cent dividend but given the expenditure on opposing the Silloth project, 3 per cent was more realistic.

The Engineer, John Dees, informed the meeting that significant work had been carried out with the portion of the line between the station at Maryport and Aspatria where the light rails had been replaced with heavy rails and this had also been the case with the section from the station to the shipping spouts at the harbour. Also included were various sidings, points and crossings.

Work was also progressing with track relaying between Wigton and Curthwaite, and rails and chairs for three miles were on order. He told the meeting that this type of work would need to be extended in the near future.

There was also still much more work to be done following the latest Act of Parliament. This involved work on the site of the proposed new station and sidings connected with the excavations for the New Dock and additional sidings on a new embankment to be made on the north side of the Wet Dock at Maryport. There was an aside that in 1850 a reserved fund of £5,505 had been created when Hudson left and his account was finally wound up and also that there had been no dividend for three years over the period when Hudson had controlled the line.

As though it seemed the issue could not entirely be laid to rest, the matter of the Silloth line came up again. The view was expressed that the Newcastle & Carlisle had dealt 'unfairly' with the Maryport & Carlisle in 'speaking against them' during the proceedings. There was also criticism about the way in which Parliament approached the matter of warring companies which could be damaging, and also the way in which plans were pruned and with a tendency to impose too many restrictions.

A comment had been made in the press that it was felt there was no real merit in the Silloth project. At a special meeting which followed, it was agreed to raise a capital of £77,712 10s. by issuing new shares with a nominal value of £12 10s.

1856

Towards the end of the year a growing concern was voiced among some of the shareholders relating to what appeared to be a falling off of traffic. This came about, it was alleged, because the local coal owners were carrying about a sixth part of their traffic free. It followed that the company was losing a sixth of this revenue due to the practice of overloading the coal wagons so that in effect a seventh wagon was not being charged. The directors were informed that this practice, contrary 'to the spirit and letter of the law', was one which was also being used on the Cockermouth & Workington Railway. There seems no evidence that the directors moved to address this complaint.

Steam and sail at the New Dock, Maryport. *Richard Stenlake Collection*

The first locomotive to be built at the railway's own works at Maryport was 2-2-2 No. 5 in 1857. *John Alsop Collection*

1857

Up to this point the locomotives being used by the company had been built by a number of external companies, mainly Tulk & Ley who had built seven of the locomotives being operated. Four had come from Hawthorns, Sharp, Stewart had provided one and E.B. Wilson had also provided one. During the year the company started to build its own locomotives and thereafter with the exception of one provided by Sharp, Stewart all the locomotives which were put into service on the line until the end of 1871 were built in the works at Maryport.

The first to be turned out from the company's own workshop in 1857 was a 2-2-2 which remained in service until 1872. There followed one built by Sharp, Stewart in the same year. Two years later, and for the following 13 years, the company built all the locomotives in their own workshop. There were 16 locomotives built during this period and although thereafter the company continued to build its own, additional ones came from other builders.

A timetable for trains from Maryport to Carlisle (but oddly not in the opposite direction!) appeared in the *Workington News* of 29th October, 1857:

	Weekdays				Sundays	
	am	am	pm	pm	am	pm
Maryport	8.00	10.29	4.30	7.35	9.20	6.40
Dearham	8.05	10.50	–	7.41	9.27	6.47
Bull Gill	8.09	10.56	4.40	7.45	9.35	6.50
Aspatria	8.22	11.14	4.49	7.54	9.50	7.00
Brayton	8.28	11.20	–	7.59	9.56?	7.10
Leegate	8.34	11.27	–	8.04	10.??	7.20
Wigton	8.46	11.38	5.10	8.20	10.10	7.30
Curthwaite	9.00	11.47	–	8.30	10.20	7.40
Dalston	9.08	11.51	5.25	8.37	10.37	7.57
Carlisle (*arrive*)	9.30	12.15	5.40	8.55	10.50	8.10

There was a Sunday service with one morning train which left Maryport at 9.20am and arrived at Carlisle at 10.50, and an evening train leaving Maryport at 6.40 and arriving at Carlisle at 8.10pm.

The railway was certainly very busy on Tuesday 20th October when the new floating dock at Maryport was opened. It was reported that 'trains from east and west poured in a vast number of visitors with some from as far away as Liverpool'.

1858

During the year there was yet another change of Secretary and General Manager when Joseph Lyndall stood down and was replaced by John Addison. The latter would 'reign' for quite a substantial period of nearly 30 years.

During March a regular passenger on the line who travelled from Dalston wrote asking why it was not possible for a fire to be kept in the waiting room during the winter months when at all the other stations comfortable fires were provided. He went so far as to enquire what the people of Dalston had done to merit this sort of treatment and to defer them from having the same comforts as were found on the other stations. It was said that enquiries had been put to the station master (who was described as a very civil and obliging man) but he could not give a satisfactory answer. There does not appear to be evidence that steps were taken to remedy this situation!

1859

In October Cummersdale station was opened to provide the facility to visit Carlisle Market because it was only open on Saturdays, market day. However, later in the year its use was extended.

1860

A change in services was announced in the local press on Saturday 1st September:

Carlisle and Allonby
Shortest route

On and after 1 September passengers will be booked through between Carlisle and Allonby and vice-versa daily by trains leaving the Citadel Station Carlisle at 10.40 am and 3.20 pm and by trains passing Aspatria for Carlisle at 11.25 am and 3.55 pm.

In the same edition just to left of this announcement there is another which is untitled. It reads,

Best route to Allonby is *via* Silloth
Leaving Canal Station at 10.15 am and 6.00 pm
Leaving Allonby at 10.00 am and 2.50 pm
The omnibus will cease running after 16th September.

Chapter Four

An increase in prosperity and further projects, 1861-1871

1861

The half-yearly meeting on Wednesday 20th February had a refreshingly optimistic air about it. The previous day in readiness for it, the directors had published their report together with the report of the auditors. Possibly with a sense of confidence, the directors expressed their 'great pleasure' meeting with the shareholders. This was because the company was showing signs of 'increased prosperity', put down to the general upturn of prosperity in the country.

The company was apparently doing so well that it was felt an extra 'engine' was going to be needed to work the increasing traffic. They emphasised that such an acquisition would be paid for out of revenue. Other projects included a carriage shed at Maryport and 'passenger sheds' at Wigton and Dalston.

There had been a slight drawback with the opening of the double track section between Wigton and Dalston following reservations by the government inspector, but the matters in question had been put in order and by the time of the meeting goods traffic had been using them for two weeks, and a week later passenger traffic had also started to do so.

There was more encouraging news insofar as there had been a great increase in the traffic at Dearham brought on the line from Broughton Moor. All in all traffic had been increasing. Needless to say this situation would suggest a healthy dividend. Yet there were some downsides.

The competition from the Silloth line, and also the line from Whitehaven to Carnforth, had had an impact on the company and it was suggested that without that the dividend might have been 10 per cent. It was said there were 'two specks on the horizon', one of which was a line being projected from Cockermouth to Keswick and then on to Penrith. It had been decided not to petition against it.

There followed a considerable amount of discussion about other possible rivals but it appears the company felt it was in a strong enough position to deal with any likely competition. However, if there were any moves to effect running powers over its line they would certainly take action to prevent that happening. It is clear that the company was now in very reliable hands with a clear sense of direction. In fact they felt able to make references to the shortcomings and lack of experience of previous Boards. In so doing, it was noted that the first eight miles of the line had cost more than the 20 miles from Aspatria to Carlisle and further, the doubling of the line had cost less than £1,600 per mile. Dividends on each share group were readily approved and it was perhaps a sign of the times that following the meeting, the shareholders dined together at 'The Golden Lion where an excellent cold collation was provided by Mrs Hayton'.

ANNO VICESIMO QUINTO & VICESIMO SEXTO

VICTORIÆ REGINÆ.

****

Cap. lxxx.

An Act to enable the *Maryport and Carlisle* Railway Company to construct Branch Railways to *Bolton* and *Wigton*, to improve their Station Accommodation at *Wigton*, to purchase additional Lands at *Wigton* and *Aikbank*, to raise further Moneys; and for other Purposes.

[30th *June* 1862.]

WHEREAS by "The *Maryport and Carlisle* Railway Act, 1855," the Acts relating to the *Maryport and Carlisle* Railway Company (in this Act called "the Company") were repealed, and were, with other Provisions, consolidated into One Act; and by that Act the Share Capital of the Company was fixed at Four hundred and twenty thousand Pounds, and they had Power to borrow One hundred and thirty-five thousand Pounds, all which Moneys have been raised and expended: And whereas it is expedient that the Company be empowered to make and maintain a Branch Railway from their Main Line of Railway at *Aspatria* to a Point at or near *Bolton*, and which Branch is herein-after called "the *Bolton* Branch Railway," and another Branch Railway from a Junction with the *Bolton* Branch Railway at or near *Mealsgate* to a Junction with the Main Line of Railway at or near *Aikbank*,

18 & 19 Vict. c. lxxix.

[*Local.*]   12 O

Soon after this meeting the directors gave notice of a special meeting to be held on Monday 15th April. There would be a request by them to the shareholders to support a proposal to build an extension to the line from Aspatria to Ireby 'and so on'. Given the general tenor of the previous meeting and manner in which there was a lot of approval for the way in which the company was being run, the decision to put forward a Bill to Parliament for an extension to their line might well have led to the conclusion that there would be no problems in getting support.

However, once again a correspondent styled simply as 'A Shareholder' was quick to write to the press. The style of writing suggests it was the same person who communicated in this manner before. In a letter to the *Carlisle Journal*, the writer told his fellow shareholders that 'the steps proposed will, if implemented, have disastrous consequences because it is like some other companies where such moves were driven by avarice or jealously'. He was of the opinion that constructing branch lines to places of small population and trade would be an error and urged the shareholders to attend the meeting and show their opposition to the proposal. It is further suggested that if the directors were so keen on building such a branch they should do it themselves.

At this special meeting the proposition was that:

> The Directors be authorized in the name and behalf of the Company to make an application to Parliament in the next ensuing session for an Act to enable the Company to make and maintain a Railway from and out of the Company's Railway at Aspatria up the Vale of Ellen by Blennerhasset and through the Bolton Coalfield in the direction of Ireby and Caldbeck. Such a proposed railway to terminate at such a point or place as in the opinion of the meeting will best serve and give accommodation to the districts of Ireby and Caldbeck until it shall be found expedient to extend the same through these districts.

A considerable amount of discussion followed, with reference made to the manner in which the company had opposed the Carlisle & Silloth Bay Railway's plan for a line from Abbey to Mealsgate. The directors seemed anxious to say that they had been considering a branch line up to the Vale of Ellen 'for some time'. There was much further discussion about the amount of traffic that would be derived from the coalfield which would 'without doubt' prove very remunerative. 'Where would the line actually terminate?' It appeared not at Mealsgate but, it was suggested, 'seemingly in a field!' The reply was that it would go further to Bolton Gate. 'What, a mile and a half after the coalfield?'

Eventually the resolution was put to the meeting and passed with only one person opposing it.

1862

Once again following this latest Bill of the previous year, another Act, Vict. cap. lxxx, was placed on the statute book. Dated 30th June, 1862, it was,

An Act to enable the *Maryport and Carlisle* Railway Company to construct Branch Railways to *Bolton* and *Wigton* to improve their Station Accommodation at *Wigton* to purchase additional Lands at *Wigton* and *Aikbank*, to raise further Moneys; and for other Purposes.

There is reference to the repealing which is stated in the Act of 1855 and the placing of all sections into one Act. It goes on to cite the expediency of empowering the company to make and maintain a branch from the 'Main Line at Aspatria' to a point near Bolton to be called 'the Bolton Branch'. There is also a further branch from a junction with this branch 'at or near' Mealsgate to a junction with the 'Main Line at or near Aikbank, to be called The Wigton Branch'. This is, in effect, one line but for logistical purposes split into two sections.

The consequence of these developments, together with other aspects, including widening the existing railway with two tracks, widening sidings, and extending coal cells at Wigton, was that permission was given to raise further capital by shares and borrowing. Much of the rest of the document sets out the terms and conditions on which this capital was to be procured. It is made clear that the 'Bolton Branch' must remain a single line.

Further, there is mention about the impact these developments will have on the roads which will be crossed by the railway when such crossings are on the same level. There should be no shunting taking place over any level crossings and trains must not be stationary on them. Where the line crossed the road in the parish of Allhallows it would be necessary to build a lodge for the gatekeeper. Section 12 of the Act makes it clear that these works had to be completed within four years otherwise permission to carry them out would lapse.

Also during this year a significant move was taken as far as motive power was concerned. By this time the locomotives were handling considerable loads and the wrought iron tyres used on them were not wearing well. For a number of years an alternative had been available which could make a considerable difference. This involved the use of steel tyres (Ahrons goes so far as to describe this change as 'the most important development in locomotive construction of the period'.) The Locomotive Superintendent at Maryport, Mr Tosh, made the decision to use this type of tyre for locomotives but he went further in the use of steel. He arranged with Adamson & Co., at Hyde, for engines to be built with steel boilers. This was an innovative step and it would seem Mr Tosh was the first Locomotive Superintendent to adopt this practice, so making the Maryport & Carlisle Railway a leader in this field.

In December further consolidation of the use of Citadel station was achieved when the Newcastle & Carlisle announced that for arrivals and departures it too would be using said station from 1st January, 1863.

It was observed that having a terminus a mile from the centre of town was a great inconvenience and mention was made that the various railway companies could never agree to join in coming to terms about the shared use. However, the amalgamation of the Newcastle & Carlisle with the North Eastern Railway made this possible because the latter, through a Parliamentary Act, was able to use Citadel station.

AN INCREASE IN PROPERTY AND FURTHER PROJECTS, 1861-1871

1864

At the half-yearly meeting in January a substantial dividend of 9 per cent was declared. On Saturday 24th September the Maryport & Carlisle Railway entered into an agreement with the Cockermouth & Workington Railway for what was termed 'traffic facilities and also running powers'. This move was made to enable the Maryport & Carlisle to move forward with another Bill. With the work listed in the Act of 1862 well under way, and with every likelihood that it would be completed within the stipulated period, the Maryport & Carlisle put another Bill before Parliament for further developments. This was drawn up and presented on Wednesday 30th November and involved a scheme to build a new branch, to be called 'The Derwent Branch'.

1865

The Act, Vict. cap. lxxxiv, dated 19th June, 1865, was to be the last Act that the company would seek. It is described as:

> An Act to enable the *Maryport and Carlisle* Railway Company to construct the *Derwent Branch* Railway, to enlarge *Bull Gill* Station, to purchase additional lands, to raise further Monies and for other Purposes.

Presumably the name derives from the proximity of the River Derwent. The Act refers to elements in the previous Act and states that the work listed there is well in hand with every indication that it would be completed in the stipulated time. Although it is not stated, it may be reasonable to assume that if this was not the case, the Bill seeking permission for further work may not have been passed to become an Act.

There is also reference to the fact that by this stage the Maryport & Carlisle had entered into an agreement with the Cockermouth & Workington Railway for traffic facilities and running powers and this necessary step for what was being proposed presumably added strength in seeking authority to build this branch.

The plan involved the branch leaving the main line of the Maryport & Carlisle at Crosby in close proximity to Bullgill station. It would terminate, in effect, with a junction on the Cockermouth & Workington line near Brigham. A request for authority to enlarge Bullgill station was approved and also the station at Brigham which had been built by the Cockermouth & Workington.

Again there is a great deal in the Act about the financial arrangements. It is stipulated that the work must be completed within three years, but it was open well within this limit.

1866

The Bolton Loop sanctioned in the Act of 1862, although a through line, was, in effect, treated as two sections. The section from Aspatria to Mealsgate opened for passengers on Monday 2nd April. The line from High Blaithwaite to

ANNO VICESIMO OCTAVO

VICTORIÆ REGINÆ.

****

Cap. lxxxiv.

An Act to enable the *Maryport and Carlisle* Railway Company to construct "The *Derwent* Branch Railway;" to enlarge the *Bull Gill* Station; to purchase additional Lands; to raise further Monies; and for other Purposes. [19th *June* 1865.]

WHEREAS by The *Maryport and Carlisle* Railway Act, 1855, the Acts relating to the *Maryport and Carlisle* Railway Company (in this Act called "the Company") were repealed, and were, with other Provisions, consolidated into One Act, and by that Act the Share Capital of the Company was fixed at Four hundred and twenty thousand Pounds, and they had Power to borrow One hundred and thirty-five thousand Pounds, all which Monies have been raised and expended: And whereas by "The *Maryport and Carlisle* Railway Act, 1862," the Company were empowered to make and maintain Branch Railways to *Bolton* and *Wigton*, and other Works, and to raise an additional Share Capital of Seventy-five thousand Pounds, and to borrow an additional Sum of Twenty thousand Pounds: And whereas the Branch Railways authorized by the Act of 1862 are now in course of Construction, and will, before the Expiration of the Year 1865, be completed and opened

18 & 19 Vict. c. lxxix.

25 & 26 Vict. c. lxxx.

AN INCREASE IN PROPERTY AND FURTHER PROJECTS, 1861-1871

Aikbank Junction was not an outstanding success. The collieries it was intended to serve failed to achieve the production levels projected and the line was seen of little use. Later developments would help to remedy this, but in the meantime it fell into disuse.

On the 13th April the following appeared in the local press,

> The Maryport and Carlisle Railway
> Through Booking
> Maryport to London
> On and after the 1st April Return Tickets
> will be issued between Maryport and London
> returning on the day of issue or on one of the three following days
>
> *By order*
> *Maryport, 27th March, 1866*

Later in this year what might have been perceived as a new challenge arose. The railway companies in west Cumberland had been, in the main, small and privately-owned. Initially their prime purpose was to facilitate the movement of coal and similar commodities. Nevertheless carrying passengers was also seen to be a means of raising significant income. Over the years it became clear that there were advantages in co-operating with other companies, for example in exercising running powers but even so when rival schemes were being promoted there could be strong opposition. However, by this time aspects in railway practice were beginning to change.

The London & North Western Railway (LNWR) was now well-established having grown from the early days and swept northwards by annexing other companies as it advanced towards its goal of establishing a link from London to Scotland. Having absorbed the Lancaster & Carlisle and, for the moment, prevented the Midland from also reaching Carlisle, it was in a strong position.

In this situation the company started to look around for further opportunities and turned its face towards west Cumberland. It shared running powers with the North Eastern Railway over the Cockermouth, Keswick & Penrith Railway (for passenger services – with the North Eastern handling freight) although this company had retained its independence and was determined to do so.

With these running powers the LNWR aimed to move further. It managed to take over the Cockermouth & Workington Railway and in so doing it reached and, further, might step over the doorstep of the Maryport & Carlisle. The previous year the Maryport & Carlisle had obtained a running agreement over the Cockermouth & Workington line on the section between Brigham to Cockermouth and also to Marron Foot. These moves had meant the LNWR had taken over this free exchange of traffic on the Cockermouth & Workington and as a result would be able to use Maryport station. This could give the LNWR the sort of foothold which might lead to it taking over the Maryport & Carlisle. There is not a great deal of clarity about what went on, if, indeed anything of significance did.

There were rumours going the rounds, and on Friday 3rd August an item featured in the *Maryport Advertiser*. It appeared in a column subheading 'Local Railways' and is more of an article than a news report. It began by stating that on the previous Wednesday (1st August) a group of directors of the LNWR had visited Maryport and had inspected the docks and the harbour. The writer goes on to say that there had been rumours for some time about a possible desire on the part of the LNWR, once it had obtained possession of the Whitehaven & Cockermouth lines, to lease the Maryport & Carlisle. Further, very advantageous terms had been offered to the shareholders in the shape of a guaranteed 10 per cent. The writer was not convinced that the move would be a good one for the local community because such a change might lead to a 'disaster' in general trade in Maryport and those who worked on the railway might be disadvantaged by such a change, not least in the wages they would receive. It was observed that, on the other hand, an influential company like the LNWR might be ready to develop the resources of the harbour, so giving a boost to the trade. In the concluding section the writer suggested it was premature to be 'counting the losses and gains of a change' and concluded with the comment: 'One thing is certain. There is a scheme of centralisation going on among the Railway Companies and it is not likely that a short line like ours can long escape contagion'. How wrong, as far as the Maryport & Carlisle Railway was concerned, would the writer prove to be!

Immediately following this article was a report on the recent Maryport & Carlisle Railway traffic returns for July: passengers, parcels, mails, horse carriages and dogs £392 15s. 6d., goods, mineral and cattle £1,130 1s. 2d. The point was made that this was considerably less than in the same period the previous year. It does not seem to be clear who, if anyone, from the Maryport & Carlisle, was involved with the visitors from the LNWR. At the end of the year a report issued contained no mention of this visit. The Maryport & Carlisle remained an independent company until government intervention in the early 1920s took away that independence.

In spite of the situation on the Bolton Loop, in December two stations were opened, Baggrow and Mealsgate. Much later, on Tuesday 1st October, 1878, High Blaithwaite was also opened on this section. Although the other two stations would remain beyond the passing of the Maryport & Carlisle, High Blaithwaite would be closed on 1st August, 1921.

1867

The final section of the line from Bullgill to Marron Junction-Broughton Cross, which had been sanctioned in the Act of 1865 was completed at the beginning of the year. On Friday 15th February it was reported in the press that the previous week a group of directors had inspected the line. A passenger train had travelled along it and all was satisfactory. However, later reports indicate that the branch was not fully opened officially until Saturday 1st June by which date the stations were opened at Papcastle (which would close on Friday 1st July, 1921), Dearham and Bullgill (both of which would survive beyond the passing of the Maryport & Carlisle).

The Derwent branch gave rise to another private station being opened on the Maryport & Carlisle, Dovenby Lodge for Dovenby Hall between Papcastle and

Dearham. The Hall was owned by Mrs Ballantine Dykes, her husband F.L.B. Dykes, Chairman of the M&CR during the 1840s, having passed away on 26th November of the previous year. It was described as 'an absolutely private one' but 'in every sense a railway station'.

With the Maryport & Carlisle obtaining running powers over the Cockermouth & Workington line, the following notice was placed in the press on 1st November, 'Passengers are now booked through between Cockermouth and Carlisle and all intermediate stations via the Bullgill and Brigham Branch'.

It would seem accidents on the line rarely happened and those which did were usually of a minor nature. However, in December there was an incident which gave rise to questions about whether a long-standing practice which had been taking place was acceptable. It was stated in a report that: 'a privilege has been allowed for many years to the collieries on the line to allow the workpeople at Rosegill, Bullgill and other pits to ride to and from work on the van attached to a mineral train'. On Friday 6th December at about 5.30pm a group of workers had boarded the van, and the train was waiting at Rosegill station so that further coal wagons could be attached. At this point a down goods train had appeared as it came around a sharp curve. Seeing it coming, the passengers in the van made an attempt to get off and although some did manage to do so before the collision, others were unable to get clear. The goods train hit the coal train with such force that at least two of the wagons fell into the River Ellen. The people who got out in time were uninjured, but those who did not suffered varying degrees of injury, although none were life threatening. The report describes the injured as being from the 'poorest class' and three of the women were said to be 'bank pickers'.

The company was quick to ensure that the injured were looked after in a period when such action was not always the case. They were provided with medical attention and Addison, the Secretary, visited each one of them and left instructions that 'everything be sent to them daily which may minister to their comfort'.

When it came to looking into the cause of this accident it was noted that there was a distant signal which should have been in use, but it had been neglected and was found not to be so. The driver of the goods train was too close to the van before he could see the next signal and by this time it was impossible to prevent the collision. He did put the locomotive into reverse but it was too late to avoid hitting the van.

The following comment was made:

> This line has been in operation upwards of thirty years and such has been the careful management of the whole line and its several branches that this is the first accident of this nature which has occurred.

1869

In the summer of 1869 there was an opportunity to have a weekend break to Liverpool by rail. It was a 'Cheap Excursion' from Maryport and calling at all stations along the line to Carlisle. This would leave Maryport at 11.25am on Saturday 26th June and the first leg of the journey would arrive in Carlisle at

1.30pm. It was at a fixed price of 6s. 6d. for what was described as 'a double journey' from all stations. What is perhaps interesting is that it was said that 'covered carriages' would be used. The return journey would leave Liverpool Lime Street station on Monday 28th June at 5.35pm, and the return train leaving Carlisle for Maryport would do so at 10.30pm. Those travelling would be allowed up to 66lb. of luggage with no extra charge but it was made clear this was taken at passengers' own risk. This, for some, would possibly be a welcome opportunity to travel to Liverpool overland rather than on one of the vessels which until now provided the only practical means of getting there.

1870

In 1870 George Tosh, the Locomotive Superintendent, who had held the position for around 16 years (there are conflicting dates relating to when he actually took up the post) relinquished this role. His contribution to the company had been outstanding, not least with the innovations he had introduced, and his legacy would be long remembered. Into his shoes stepped Hugh Smellie who would continue to run the department until 1878.

By now the state of the track on the Aikbank section of the Bolton Loop was in such a state of deterioration that it was removed.

A less than reverential depiction of the Maryport & Carlisle on this commercial postcard. *Author's Collection*

Chapter Five

Improvements in operations, 1872-1900

1872

Since 1857 the company had been building its own locomotives and it also bought in locomotives from other manufacturers. In the period 1872-1873 four from Beyer, Peacock were purchased. The company continued to build as well with three locomotives turned out in 1873. In 1874, after 24 years as Chairman, G.W. Hartley stood down and Sir Wilfrid Lawson of Brayton Hall took on the role, which he held until 1906.

At the half-yearly meeting in June 1876 those present were informed of the problems which had arisen following the iron trade in west Cumberland suffering depression. In spite of this it was possible to have a dividend of 11 per cent. It was reported that in the previous January 'the locomotive establishment at Bog Station Carlisle was moved to Currock Junction'.

A rule book, issued in this period, indicates that at the time the company was using a signalling system which used three positions. 'Danger' was indicated by the arm being horizontal and in addition at night a red light would be visible. 'Caution' would see the arm being at an angle of 45 degrees down from the horizontal position and be accompanied by a green light. When the line was clear the arm would drop further to align with the signal post and a white light would be visible. In some places disc signals were being used as well. However, in the early part of 1877 the Board of Trade ruled that the signalling system must be brought up to the required standard and it was reported at the first half-yearly meeting in February that the cost of installing interlocking signals was £3,000, rather more than the company had anticipated. On the other hand there had been more coal depots needed at Wigton, reflecting a growth in traffic and revenue.

1878-1899

In 1878 Hugh Smellie gave up the role of Locomotive Superintendent. He was, in effect, returning 'home' in rejoining the Glasgow & South Western Railway where he had trained before being appointed by the Maryport & Carlisle. Robert Campbell became the new Locomotive Superintendent on the Maryport & Carlisle.

At the half-yearly meeting held on Thursday, 24th January, 1878, the Chairman was able to inform those present that 'everything has gone very satisfactorily and there was nothing to which he would draw special attention'. Traffic rates had now doubled. He commented it was pleasing to see that problems in Europe (relating to revolts and war against the Ottoman Empire and the meeting of European powers in Berlin to settle these problems) were being resolved. They had had something of an impact on the company but once

Maryport & Carlisle Ry. — MARYPORT to CARLISLE.

	WEEK DAYS.										SUNDAYS		
	mrn	mrn	mrn	A	aft	aft	aft				mrn	aft	aft
Whitehaven .... dep	6 25	8 0	1020	1 10	2 30	5 10	6 45	..			8 45	5 10	..
MARYPORT .... ,,	7 5	8 40	11 3	1 48	3 10	6 0	7 23	..			9 30	5 55	..
Dearham Bridge	7 11	8 46	..	1 54	..	6 6	7 29	..			9 36	6 1	..
Bull Gill .... arr	7 15	8 50	1110	1 58	3 17	6 10	7 33	..			9 40	6 5	..
23 Derwent Branch { Cockermouth ...... dep	..	8 15	1040	1 25	2 45	5 40	7 5				8 55	5 35	7 50
Brigham	..	8 21	1046	1 31	2 51	5 46	7 11				9 1	5 41	7 56
Papcastle	*	*	*	*	*	*	*				*	*	*
Dearham	..	8 33	1059	1 44	3 4	5 59	7 24		Stops on Tuesdays only.	Stops at Leegate on Wednesdays only.	9 14	5 54	8 9
Bull Gill	..	8 39	11 5	1 50	3 10	6 5	7 30				9 20	6 0	8 15
Dearham Bridge	..	*	*	..	*	..	*				9 34	*	*
Maryport .... arr	..	8 51	1120	2 17	3 25	6 35	7 45				9 40	6 15	8 30
Bull Gill for Carlisle .. dep	7 17	8 52	1112	2 0	3 19	6 12	7 35	..			9 42	6 7	..
Aspatria (Allonby) .... arr	7 23	8 58	1118	2 6	3 25	6 18	7 41	..			9 49	6 14	..
B'lt'n Loop line. { Aspatria .... dep	7 30	..	..	2 15	4 20	6 22	..	..			..	..	..
Baggrow	7 38	..	..	2 23	4 28	6 30	..	..			..	..	..
Mealsgate .... arr	7 45	..	..	2 30	4 35	6 37	..	..			..	..	..
Aspatria for Carlisle ....dep	7 25	9 0	1120	2 8	3 26	6 20	7 43				9 50	6 15	..
Brayton	7 30	9 5	1125	2 13	3 31	6 25	7 48				9 55	6 20	..
Leegate	7 36	9 11	B	2 19	C	6 31	..				10 1	6 26	..
Wigton	7 45	9 20	1138	2 28	3 44	6 40	8 1				1010	6 35	..
Curthwaite	7 54	9 29	1147	2 37	3 52	6 49	8 10				1019	6 44	..
Dalston	8 0	9 35	1154	2 44	4 0	6 56	8 17	..			1025	6 50	..
Cummersdale	8 7	9 43	12 1	2 51	..	7 3	..	..			1033	6 58	..
CARLISLE .... arr	8 13	9 50	12 8	2 58	4 10	7 10	8 27	..			1040	7 5	..

* Calls when required on notice being given at the preceding Stopping Station.
A.—Runs on Mondays only between Cockermouth and Maryport.

Maryport & Carlisle Ry. — CARLISLE to MARYPORT.

	WEEK DAYS.								SUNDAYS		
	mrn	mrn	A	aft	aft	aft		aft		mrn	mrn	aft
CARLISLE .... dep	6 40	9 10	1045	1 15	3 30	5 35	..	9 0	..	..	8 30	6 10
Cummersdale	6 45	9 15	1050	1 20	3 35	C	..	9 5	..	..	8 35	6 15
Dalston	6 51	9 21	1056	1 26	3 41	5 44	..	9 11	..	..	8 41	6 21
Curthwaite	6 57	9 27	11 2	1 32	3 47	5 50	..	9 17	..	..	8 47	6 27
Wigton	7 7	9 37	1112	1 41	3 57	5 59	..	9 26	..	..	8 57	6 37
Leegate	7 14	B	1120	..	4 5	..	..	9 33	..	..	9 5	6 45
Brayton	7 20	9 48	1127	1 53	4 12	6 11	..	9 39	..	..	9 12	6 52
Aspatria (Allonby)........arr	7 24	9 52	1131	1 57	4 16	6 15	..	9 43	..	..	9 16	6 56
B lt'n Loop line. { Mealsgate ...... dep	7 3	..	1055	..	3 55	5 55	..	..	..		..	..
Baggrow	7 10	..	11 2	..	4 2	6 2	..	..	..		..	..
Aspatria........... arr	7 17	..	11 8	..	4 8	6 8	..	..	..		..	..
Aspatria, for Maryport dep	7 26	9 53	1133	1 59	4 18	6 17	..	9 44	..	..	9 17	6 57
Bull Gill .... arr	7 33	10 0	1140	2 0	4 25	6 24	..	9 51	..	..	9 24	7 4
23 Derwent Branch { Maryport .... dep	7 30	9 55	1135	1 48	4 20	6 0	..	..	..	8 0	9 0	7 0
Dearham Bridge	*	*	*	1 54	*	6 6	..	..	..	*	9 36	*
Bull Gill for C'rmouth	7 40	10 6	1150	2 7	4 34	6 26	..	..	..	8 15	9 45	7 18
Dearham	7 45	1011	1156	2 13	4 40	6 32	..	..	..	8 21	9 51	7 24
Papcastle	*	*	*	*	*	*	..	..	..	*	*	*
Brigham	7 58	1024	1210	2 26	4 53	6 45	..	..	..	8 34	10 4	7 37
Cockermouth ...... arr	8 4	1030	1216	2 32	4 59	6 51	..	..	..	8 40	1010	7 43
Bull Gill for Maryport ..dep	7 36	10 2	1142	2 9	4 27	6 27	..	9 52	..	..	9 26	7 6
Dearham Bridge	7 43	10 9	1149	..	4 34	..	..	9 59	..	..	9 35	7 14
MARYPORT .... arr	7 50	1015	1155	2 17	4 40	6 35	..	10 5	..	..	9 40	7 20
Whitehaven .... ,,	8 35	1055	1235	2 45	5 25	7 10	..	1035	..		1020	8 5

A.—Runs on Mondays only between Maryport & C'rmouth. C.—Stops on Saturdays.
B.—Stops at Leegate on Fridays.

Maryport & Carlisle Railway timetable, July 1893.

peace had been restored he was sure there would be a revival of trade and he was optimistic industry would prosper. In spite of this he could announce a dividend of 12 per cent. He was happy to say there had been no division on the Board for 10 years. There had been the chance to increase the engine accommodation at Carlisle station and new sidings would now be needed. He spoke about the possible introduction of the block system on the line but concluded that because all the trains stopped at every station, the block system did not seem to be appropriate for the M&CR. However, they would look into it. He felt the platform at Maryport needed to be made larger, together with the station buildings and these actions were to be considered.

The directors then decided to seek authorisation to make application to the Board of Trade to raise £70,500 by issuing new shares and £23,500 by borrowing on a mortgage, 'this was in view of the continued expenditure on the capital account in providing accommodation for the traffic'. This was carried and existing shareholders would have preference.

Towards the end of 1878 the collieries at the top end of the Bolton Loop were active enough to justify the reopening of the section of line intended to serve them and the line was brought back into use at the beginning of October. There would be further vacillations over the use of this section of the loop in the years ahead.

In 1885, after a substantial period of years, John Addison handed over the baton of Secretary and General Manager to Hugh Carr who would be the penultimate holder of the title.

As methods in the iron and steel industry changed, the exchanges of ore, coal and coke between east and west became less necessary and this had an impact on the revenues of those railway companies such as the Eden Valley Railway and the Cockermouth, Keswick & Penrith Railway. This was also the case with the Maryport & Carlisle and at the half-yearly meeting on Wednesday 18th August, 1886, the Chairman, Sir Wilfrid Lawson, said that he 'deplored' the considerable falling off in the receipts 'owing mainly to the coke traffic from the north-eastern district being considerably less'.

He announced that their revenue was £4,584 less, and even on the passenger side there had been a decrease of 11,287 passengers carried. The proposal was to adopt a dividend of 6¾ per cent.

During the 1890s the station building at Wigton, constructed of Cumberland dressed sandstone, was dismantled and replaced with a new structure, with a grander platform and canopy. Some of the stone from the original building was acquired by Maryport & Carlisle shareholder Humphrey Senhouse and it was used to construct a summer house on his private estate. He took four columns and capitals, much of the dressed plinths and stonework as well as two of the four pediments. Some 130 years later the summer house was in a poor state of repair, although one pediment was virtually intact. This was removed in April 2022 and is now on public display in West Avenue, Wigton.

In 1896 Dovenby Lodge station was made available for use by the public. In 1898 William Coulthard was appointed Locomotive Superintendent and replaced William Robinson who had been in post from 1893.

The original, rather grandiose, station building at Wigton *circa* 1890. The building was soon to be replaced with a new structure. *G. Biddle Collection/Kidderminster Railway Museum*

This line drawing depicts the pattern on the original Wigton station sign which was carved in stone. *Thelma Western*

Chapter Six

The company's final years, 1900-1923

The turn of the century initially brought little in the way of significant changes although as it progressed there would be challenging situations and a surprise development. It was in 1900 that the company built its last locomotive. There would be three more put into service in this period before the demise of the company. One of these would be built by the North British Locomotive Co. and two by the Yorkshire Engine Co.

In keeping up with the excursion element there was, in August 1906, an announcement for the annual excursion to Liverpool, Manchester and Belle Vue Gardens. These were for one, three, six or 12 days and ran on 3rd September. The train would leave Maryport at 11.50pm (Sunday).

In 1904 J.B. Adamson became the last Locomotive Superintendent for the line.

1905-1912

In 1905 the decision was made to effect a change in some of the liveries. Perhaps this might have been seen as giving a boost to the image. There is no indication that the liveries of the locomotives were to be changed, they were painted green with black bands lined with vermillion. Up to this point the carriages, mainly of the four-wheeled variety, had a fairly uninspiring coat of varnished teak and the lettering was in gold. The new look had two panels. The lower section was now painted dark green whilst the upper section was painted in white with what was described as having 'a faint greenish tinge'. To make the whole look even more striking gold paint was used to give stripes round such places as the windows and the panels. The goods wagons were not overlooked either. They also appeared more striking, after being painted in what was described as a 'lead' colour with the lettering painted white.

The year 1906 saw a change of Chairman. It was now the turn of Thomas Hartley of Armathwaite Hall who would be the last to hold the office and would do so until the company's demise in 1922. In all there would be only five Chairmen in the whole of the company's existence. Hartley would have to deal with changing times.

On Sunday 1st November, 1908 Linefoot station was closed, the last station closure during the company's existence. It was also in 1908 that Thomas Blain took over the position of Secretary and General Manager. He was the last person to hold the position as a joint post and would be there at the demise of the company.

At the half-yearly meeting the following year, held at the Station House on Wednesday 24th February, 1909 the Chairman had a great deal to say about a number of issues affecting the railway and its future. To begin, a dividend of just 6 per cent was proposed but following his explanation about significant steps being considered there seemed to be a general acceptance by the shareholders of the situation. The lower dividend resulted mainly from a loss of

An extract from *Bradshaw's Guide* of April 1910 showing M&CR passenger trains.

A Maryport & Carlisle Railway document dated May 1912.

traffic and might have been lower still had they not kept expenses as low as possible.

It was reported that during the half-year ending 31st December, 1908 there had been 13,000 passenger journeys fewer than the number in the same period in 1907 and this decrease involved all classes but especially third class. Merchandise receipts were also down by £1,740, brought about to a large extent by the reduction in the tonnage carried of items such as steel rails, pig iron and scrap iron from the furnaces in west Cumberland. Whereas the revenue from the carriage of livestock had seen an increase, that of mineral traffic had shown a dramatic decline and was down by £4,124. This latter slump was put down to the severe depression in the west Cumberland iron and steel trade with fewer furnaces operating. What had made the situation even worse was the strike at the Allhallows Colliery, the outcome being that less coal was carried. Added to this was the closure of a local limestone quarry. In all the Maryport & Carlisle had worked some 21,910 train miles fewer.

All this was on the down side and it was felt there must be a move to develop the running of the line to make it more attractive, especially when it came to the passenger traffic. It appears there was a more positive attitude here than there had been on occasions in the past when things were not going well.

The meeting was informed that the decision had been made to convert a number of third class carriages into workman's carriages and to fit two passenger trains with L'Techs incandescent lighting, a system of lighting which, it was felt, would probably find the approval of everybody travelling on the line. The M&CR would also use this system to improve the lighting at Currock yard in Carlisle which would mean that any men working there on shunting operations would be less at risk.

Another point was raised, and the view expressed, that it was rather hard on passengers arriving at Carlisle in the steam-heated carriages of the trains on the main line, to then get into the cold carriages of the Maryport & Carlisle line, especially in the early morning. The best available at present was the use of foot warming pans. These could prove troublesome and were ineffective because only two people in the carriage could make use of one. In view of this the decision was made to fit passenger trains with steam heating. This raised a cheer from those present. The cost would be about £1,000.

There were plans to build more houses for the employees and a move to expand the facilities at the Elizabeth Dock. Also the company's three burries were in need of replacement. The reason for this was that the chaldron wagons used on the line were antiquated and needed to be replaced by the larger 10-ton wagons which were too big for using with the burries for shipping coal. Money would have to be spent in carrying out these changes.

The meeting seemed to go along with all this and the only issue which some had was that the present timetable provided an inadequate service in the evening from Carlisle. It was felt that there were too many trains in the afternoon and then no trains between 5.35pm and 9.00pm.

On Monday 26th March, 1911 the following report appeared in the *Hartlepool Northern Daily Mail*.

The M&CR's three-road Currock engine shed at Carlisle *circa* 1905. The locomotives in view are 2-4-0 No. 8 of 1876 and 0-4-2 No. 4 of 1879. Both of these veterans were to survive into LMS days where they became Nos. 10006 and 10010 respectively. *Author's Collection*

Coal traffic formed a vital part of the traffic and revenue for the Maryport & Carlisle Railway. At the head of a lengthy train is 0-6-0 No. 19 with a train of coal empties near Carlisle.
Author's Collection

A man of unknown identity threw himself in front of a passenger train on the Maryport and Carlisle Railway half a mile west of Wigton yesterday. The engine driver was helpless because the man sprung from behind a buttress and met his fate in an instant. A short time previously the man, when standing on the bridge over the railway asked two men who were passing what horse had won the Grand National. On being told, he looked disappointed.

At the half-yearly meeting held on Wednesday 21st February, 1912, the Chairman announced that the directors proposed to spend £600 on the capital account at Wigton. The Chairman said they 'were loath to spend a half-penny more on the Capital Account than absolutely necessary but there had been complaints from Wigton'. There was a need for more shed accommodation and the members of staff were finding it impossible to cope with the increased traffic. The Chairman felt it would be foolish for the directors to shut their eyes to this fact. He suggested it was clear they must not lose the chance of any traffic or allow traffic to be spoiled by exposure to weather. The total loss of revenue reported was £4,935 from every source. Expenditure to stations had been £153 more and had involved alterations and enlargements to Crown Street coal yard at Carlisle and improvements at Wigton station.

The directors had come to the conclusion that first class fares were so low that they could not reduce them. Once again it was only possible to have a dividend of 6 per cent on ordinary shares.

1913

The timetable for April gives details of a substantial service:

Leaves Carlisle (Weekdays)

					TSO					
Carlisle	6.40	9.10		10.45	1.30	3.35	4.00	5.30	7.30	9.05
Cummersdale	6.45	9.15		10.50	1.35	3.40		5.35	7.35	9.10
Dalston	6.51	9.21		10.56	1.41	3.45	4.10	5.41		9.14
Curthwaite	6.57	9.27		11.02	1.47	3.52		5.48	7.47	9.22
Wigton	7.07	9.37		11.11	1.57	4.00	4.21	5.56	7.57	9.31
Leegate	7.14			11.18	2.04			6.03		*
Brayton	7.20	9.48		11.25	2.10		4.32	6.09		9.42
Aspatria	7.26	9.53		11.30	2.16		4.38	6.15		9.47
Bullgill	7.36	8.40	10.02	11.09	11.37	2.25		4.46	6.24	7.34
Dearham Bridge	7.43	8.45	10.09	11.14	11.44	2.33			6.30	7.40 10.00
Maryport	7.50	8.51	10.15	11.20	11.50	2.40		4.53	6.36	7.45 10.05

* Stops when required. TSO – Tuesday and Saturday only.

On Sundays there were two trains, one in the morning leaving Carlisle at 8.45 and arriving at Maryport at 9.55 and the other in the evening leaving Carlisle at 5.20 and arriving at Maryport at 6.30. Both trains stopped at all stations.

A northbound goods train departs from Wigton station as smoke rises from the chimney of the jam factory in the distance. This image has been reproduced to a larger size on the inside cover.
Richard Stenlake Collection

Publicity to promote through travel over the Maryport & Carlisle Railway as the 'Best and most direct route'. See also the map on page 4.
Author's Collection

THE COMPANY'S FINAL YEARS, 1900-1923

Leaves Maryport   TO

Maryport	7.05	7.20	8.40	9.55	11.00	11.35	2.05		4.25	6.00	7.26	9.45
Dearham Bridge	7.11	7.25	8.46	10.00		11.40	2.11		4.30	6.06	7.32	9.51
Bullgill	7.17	7.30	8.52	10.05	11.08	11.45	2.16		4.37	6.13	7.38	9.57
Aspatria	7.25		9.00		11.15		2.24		4.44	6.20	7.46	10.05
Brayton	7.30		9.05		11.20		2.29		4.49	6.25	7.51	10.10
Leegate	7.36		9.11		11*t*25		2.35			6.31		10.16
Wigton	7.45		9.20		11.32		2.44	4.10	5.00	6.40	8.04	10.25
Curthwaite	7.54		9.29		11.40		2.53	4.19	5.08	6.49	8.13	10.34
Dalston	8.00		9.35		11.46		3.00	4.25	5.16	6.56	8.20	10.40
Cummersdale	8.07		9.43				3.07	4.33		7.03		10.48
Carlisle	8.13		9.50		11.55		3.14	4.38	5.25	7.10	8.30	10.55

t – Tuesday. TO – Tuesdays only

On Sundays there were two trains. The first left Maryport in the morning at 9.45 and reached Carlisle at 10.55. The other left Maryport in the evening at 5.50 and arrived in Carlisle at 7.02. Both trains stopped at all stations.

1914

World War I (1914-1918) brought many changes for the railway companies. The Powers of the Regulation of the Forces Act 1871 allowed the railways to be put under the control of the government. The resulting aftermath following the war would lead to a radical re-organisation of the national railway system. The regulation was invoked on 4th August, 1914 and it was decided that dividends for a particular railway company during the war whilst under government control would be based on the performance of the previous year, 1913. However, in the case of the Maryport & Carlisle this appears not to have been strictly applied because although the dividend in 1913 was 6½ per cent it was dropped in 1914 to 5 per cent and remained so until 1917 when it went up to 5½ per cent. It remained at that level until and including 1920, dropping in 1921 to 4½ per cent.

Post-World War I

On Monday 1st August, 1921 the line from High Blaithwaite to Aikbank Junction was again closed, although in September it was reopened for goods traffic. It remained open after the Maryport & Carlisle had ceased to exist.

The government's control of the railways during the war had meant that little had been done in the way of maintenance and repair. There was some doubt about where the situation was leading because there seemed, after the war, some hesitancy in the move by the government to return the railway companies to their rightful owners. At one point there had been a feeling some form of nationalisation might be introduced but that would have placed a heavy financial burden on government which would not only be faced with compensating the companies but also with the cost of bringing the system back to some sort of reasonable operational level. Nevertheless the boards of many companies began to be concerned about why the government was being so slow to act.

Horse and handler at Maryport Horse Show, with the railway and a rake of passenger stock in the background.
John Alsop Collection

The date and reason for this visit of dignitories to Brayton Junction is not known. Presumably it was some sort of inspection party.
John Alsop Collection

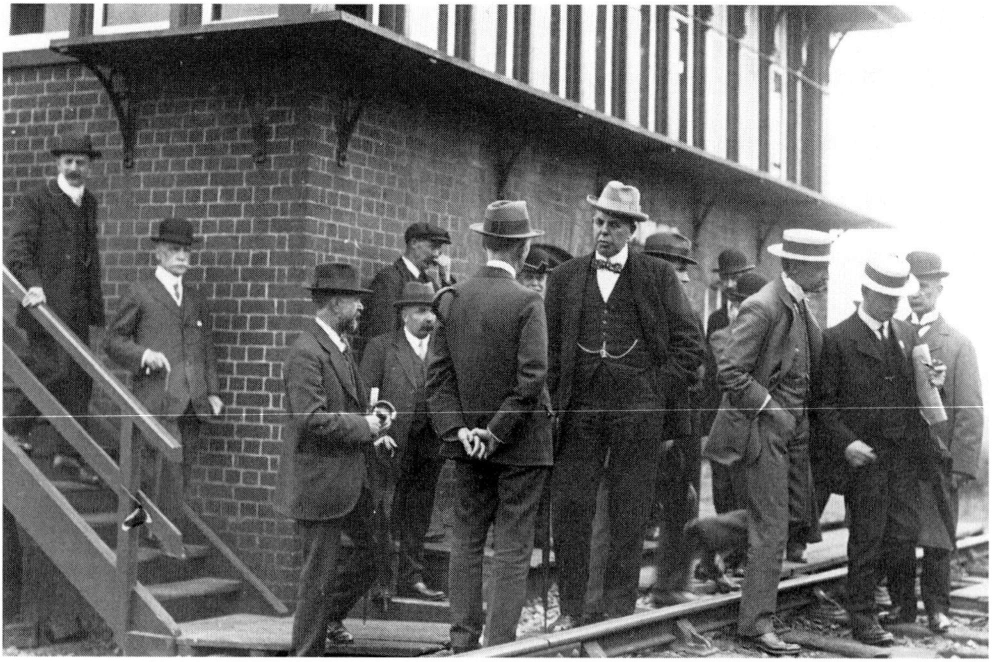

THE COMPANY'S FINAL YEARS, 1900-1923

Eventually it became clear what the future would hold. The plan was to merge all the companies into four main regional groups, what became known as the 'Grouping'. For some there had already been close co-operation which barely fell short of amalgamation, but for others who had fiercely maintained their independence, and the Maryport & Carlisle was amongst these, it would mean the end of their existence.

At a meeting on 20th July, 1920 the directors issued a statement to the effect that in view of the state of trade and the uncertain outlook caused by government control of the railways coming to an end on 14th August the interim dividend payable for the half-year ending on 30th June, 1920 would be reduced to four per cent, a drop from the interim five per cent in the previous years. The government then moved ahead with the plans for these amalgamations and in 1922 the final arrangements were made.

In 1923 the Maryport & Carlisle Railway passed into history, having been absorbed into one of the new 'Big Four', namely the London, Midland & Scottish Railway. Some 29 Maryport & Carlisle Railway locomotives went into the use of this new group with numbers being given in the ranges 10xxx, 11xxx and 12xxx. The oldest of these had been built at Maryport in 1865. Its rebuild in 1907 enabled a further 20 years service before withdrawal.

Postscript

The Maryport & Carlisle Railway was remarkable not least for what may be described as a 'parochial', some have said 'feudal', venture epitomised by the way in which certain locomotives were named after some of the local worthies who had been involved in building it, and their use of private stations.

Yet later, when lines in this area and indeed elsewhere, which had started as private ventures and when much later rationalisation began to bite, were closed down, part of the former Maryport & Carlisle Railway remained. This is because it became a key part of the line following the west coast of what was formerly Cumberland, now part of Cumbria, and it remains very much the case today.

A memorial plaque to the Maryport & Carlisle railwaymen lost during World War I. Originally sited at Maryport station, it is seen here in the Memorial Gardens, Maryport in 1995.
J. Marshall Collection/ Kidderminster Railway Museum

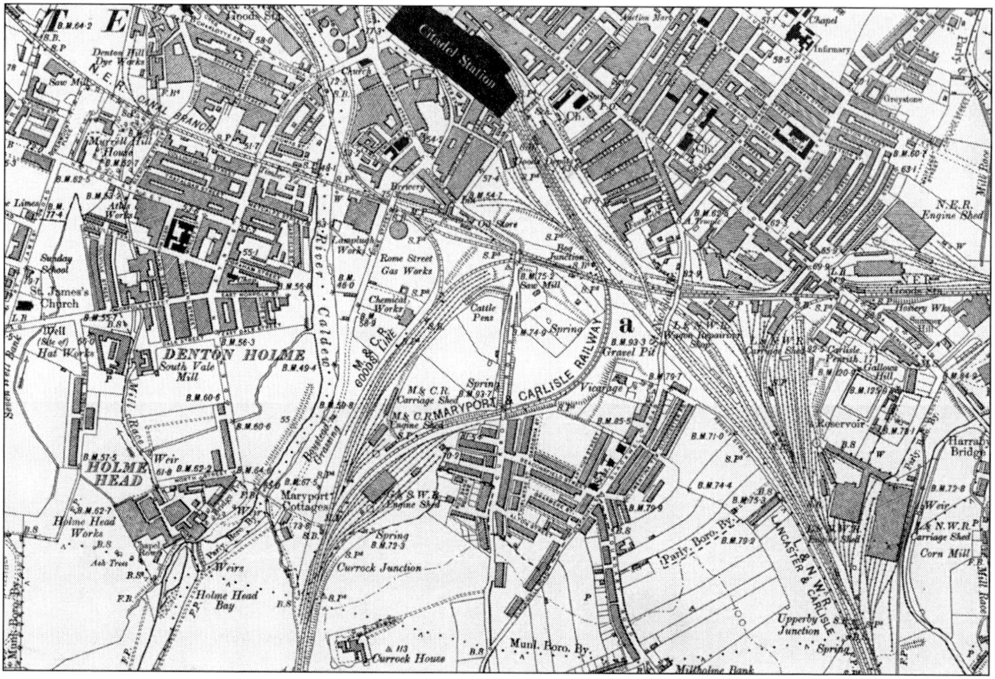

Map showing the lines south of Carlisle Citadel station (*centre top*). The LNWR West Coast Main Line approaches from the bottom right, and the Newcastle & Carlisle line enters the city from centre right. The M&CR main line departs south from Citadel, before sweeping south-westerly towards Currock Junction. As Currock Junction is approached the Maryport & Carlisle Railway engine shed is on the right and the Glasgow & South Western Railway shed on the left.

Reproduced from the 6in. Ordnance Survey map of 1899

M&CR 2-4-0 No. 8 stands beneath the train shed at Carlisle Citadel *circa* 1900. The locomotive was built at Maryport in 1876 and rebuilt in 1895. *Kidderminster Railway Museum Collection*

Chapter Seven

Description of the line

In this chapter we trace a journey from Carlisle Citadel to Maryport *circa* 1900, before turning our attention to the Bolton Loop (Aikbank Junction to Aspatria via Mealsgate), and the Derwent branch (Bullgill to Brigham).

On leaving Citadel station, our train heads south, before it turns in a south-westerly direction. It passes between the locomotive shed of the Maryport & Carlisle Railway on the right and the more substantial sheds of the Glasgow & South Western Railway on the left.

It then turns in a southerly direction through Currock Junction and past Currock House as it continues to follow a southerly direction to reach Cummersdale where it crosses the River Caldew on an iron bridge. The line travels adjacent to the dye works which supplies the nearby mills. Here there is a station. Then the line passes through 'the very beautiful valley' of the Caldew and eventually, after about 3½ miles, it reaches the station at Dalston, a comparatively small community at this time.

Moving on, the line passes westwards for a short distance before turning back in a south-westerly direction and then turns west at Curthwaite station. It continues in this direction to pass near Crofton Hall and Crofton station. This is a private station, about which one writer commented that it 'is not one of the prettiest of stations when compared with the other private stations to be found on this line'. This judgement is perhaps a little harsh; see the photograph on page 79.

Having travelled a distance of about 11 miles, our train reaches Wigton station. A replacement station building had been built in the 1890s. Wigton has a rich history stretching back through the period of the Roman occupation. For a time it was part of Scotland and possibly this is why it is not listed in the *Domesday Book*. It is said that the name derives from 'Wicga's tun' which denotes a hamlet belonging to Wicga. Significant siding accommodation is available to deal with local industry. Within the immediate environs of the station there is a coal depot, a timber yard and saw mills, a livestock market, a tannery, dye works, a flour mill and jam factories.

Moving on, the line turns in a more southerly direction, and passes near the Brookfield Academy, belonging to the Society of Friends. It once had a station but this was closed in 1845.

After passing a brick and tile works, the line now heads in a more westerly direction. At just over 13 miles into the journey, we reach Aikbank Junction and here a branch goes off in a south-easterly direction. This junction is the northern end of the first appendage to the line and referred to as the 'Bolton Loop'. After this, the main line continues in a south-westerly direction to Leegate station and thereafter, once again, it passes through open countryside through Low Row where the traveller might well notice that farming is the predominant activity in the area. In a short while the line goes near to Brookfield and Brayton Hall, the latter being the seat of Sir Wilfrid Lawson, Baronet.

The classic view of a Maryport & Carlisle Railway passenger service departing Carlisle Citadel. The train is being hauled by 0-4-2 No. 5, originally built at Maryport in 1873, and subsequently rebuilt. *John Alsop Collection*

Carlisle Crown Street coal yard and goods depot in July 1955. The approach road from Crown Street passes alongside the good shed. Crown Street itself passed beneath the main line at the southern end of Citadel station (*see map page 74*). Carlisle Citadel station is seen in the background on the right. *John Alsop Collection*

Maryport Cottages, Carlisle, in March 2000. These terraced houses were built by the Maryport & Carlisle for its railwaymen and their families and are marked on the Ordnance Survey map on page 74. They are to the west of the M&CR line, almost opposite the Glasgow & South Western Railway engine shed.

G. Biddle/ Kidderminster Railway Museum

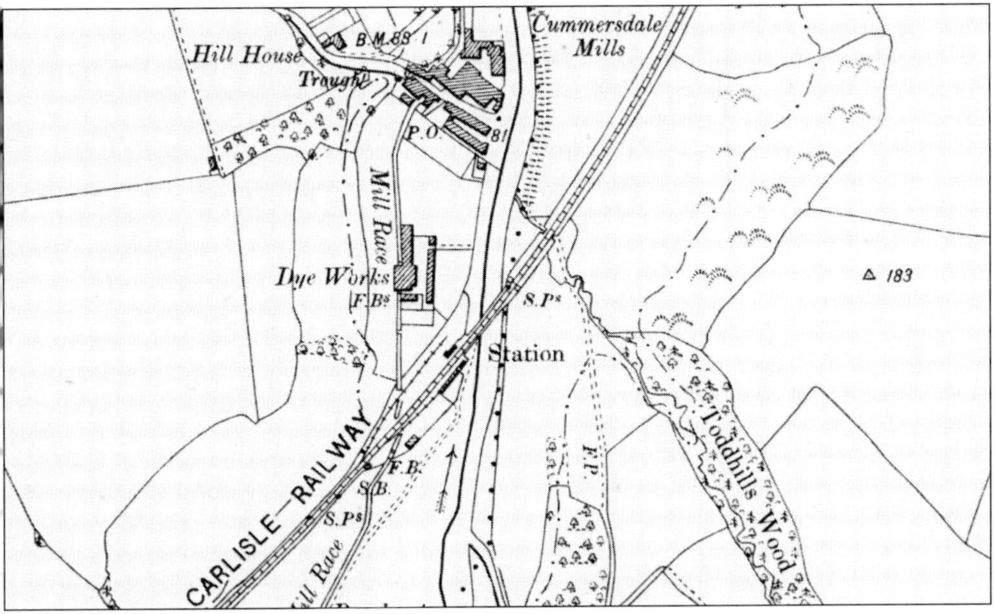

ALONG THE LINE IN THE LATE 19TH CENTURY

Cummersdale station. *Reproduced from the 6in. Ordnance Survey map of 1899*

Cummersdale station, looking towards Carlisle on 9th May, 1966. The station looks to be in surprisingly good order, having closed to passengers on 18th June, 1951. At this date it remained open to goods traffic before succumbing completely on 6th March, 1961. *John Alsop*

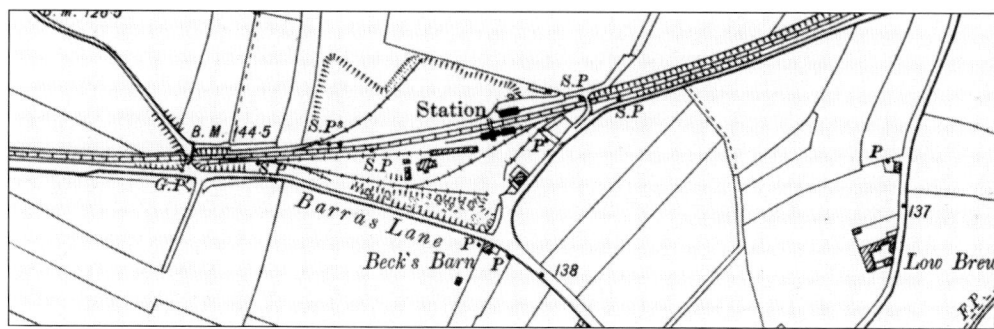

Dalston station.
Reproduced from the 6in. Ordnance Survey map of 1899

Dalston station *circa* 1920, with 2-4-0 No. 8 on a southbound (down) train.
Author's Collection

The good shed at Dalston was adjacent to the station's southbound platform.
SLS Collection

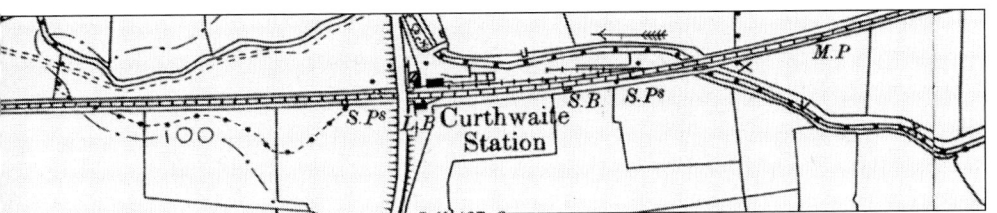

Curthwaite station.
Reproduced from the 6in. Ordnance Survey map of 1899

Curthwaite station, view looking towards Maryport.
John Alsop Collection

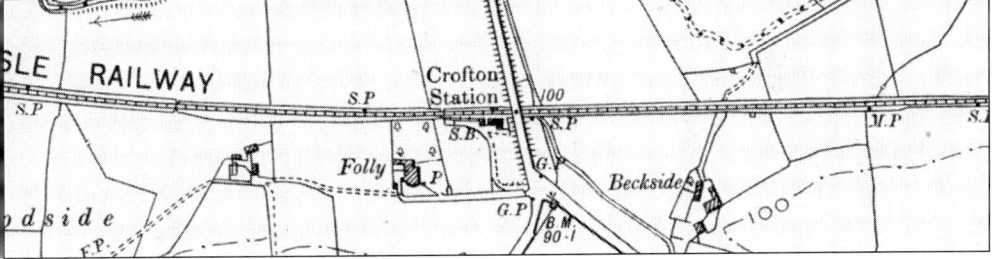

Crofton station.
Reproduced from the 6in. Ordnance Survey map of 1899

Crofton private station, view looking towards Carlisle. The station was built for the Brisco family, who are standing on the down platform in this *circa* 1900 view.
G. Biddle Collection/ Kidderminster Railway Museum

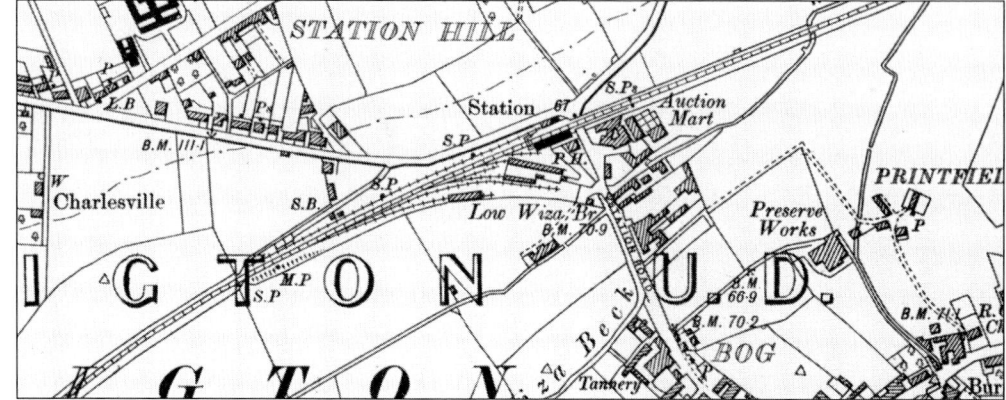

There were major developments at Wigton station in the early years of the 20th century, as can be seen by comparing the 1899 6 inch survey (*above*) and the 1924 25 inch map (*below*). Note the large rail-connected jam factory alongside the goods yard on the latter.

Reproduced from Ordnance Survey maps

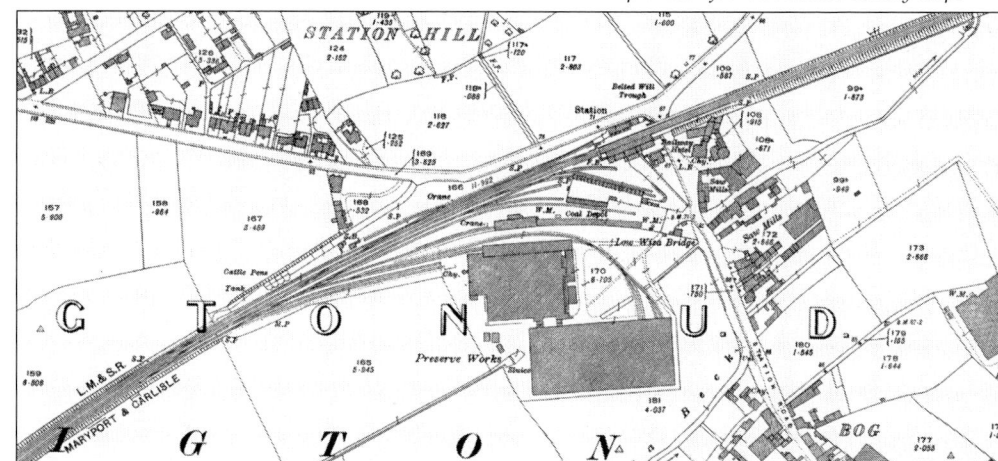

A 1967 view at Wigton looking towards Carlisle. The station building replaced the earlier structure illustrated on page 64. On 15th August, 1918, some 500 employees from the jam factory gathered on the station platform. As a train backed down there was a crush and some fell onto the track. Fortunately none of the injuries sustained resulted in fatality.

R.E.G. Read/ Kidderminster Railway Museum

There is then Brayton Junction where the branch of the Kirtlebridge, Annan & Brayton Railway heads off northwards. Shortly afterwards, the train reaches Brayton station, once private but opened to the public in 1848. The Caledonian Railway also has the use of Brayton station as it is the endpoint for services on the Kirtlebridge/Solway Junction line. The woodland immediately south of the station is known as Station Wood while to the north of the line there is a reservoir within Carr Wood. Brayton station is soon followed by Brayton Domain Colliery with its many sidings and this is where the line begins to enter coal mining territory. This colliery is served by the railway.

The line continues once again in a south-westerly direction, and immediately after passing over the junction which gives access to the southern end of the Bolton Loop, which merges from our left, we arrive at Aspatria station which has been built in the Tudor Gothic style, very popular in this period. Our train has covered about 18½ miles.

Travelling on, the line skirts close to Nether Hall, the residence of J.P. Senhouse, another personality associated with promoting the building of this railway and the M&CR's first Chairman. The Senhouse family were very influential in the district. Then the journey continues to take a south-westerly direction and then turns westerly and passes Oughterside Mill. Bullgill Colliery is next on the line where there is also a station. Bullgill became the junction for the Derwent branch on its opening in 1867. From our train, some disused collieries will be noticed, and among these is Crosby Colliery. The line also passes the disused Rosegill Colliery.

The train then reaches Dearham Bridge station (known simply as Dearham until 1867) where there is an adjoining mineral line going off which serves Crosshaw Colliery. Here there is an abandoned mineral line going off to Dearham Hall. In a short section, now running westerly, the train runs close to the River Ellen before turning south-westwards again.

The journey, after some 26 miles, ends with arrival at Maryport with its 'splendid station'. The line continues from Maryport station to the harbour with its maze of sidings. Like some other Cumberland towns, Maryport has connections with the Roman occupation. Established around 122AD as Alauna, there was a Roman road that linked it to Derventio (Papcastle). Subsequently the town became known as Ellenfoot and it only gained the name Maryport later. Humphrey Senhouse, responsible for much of the development of the port and the shipbuilding, together with associated industries including coalmining, decided to rename it after his wife Mary. He linked her name with the main feature of the town to immortalise her memory as Maryport. It became a vibrant industrial town centred around the port. The coming of the railway did much to enhance this prosperity.

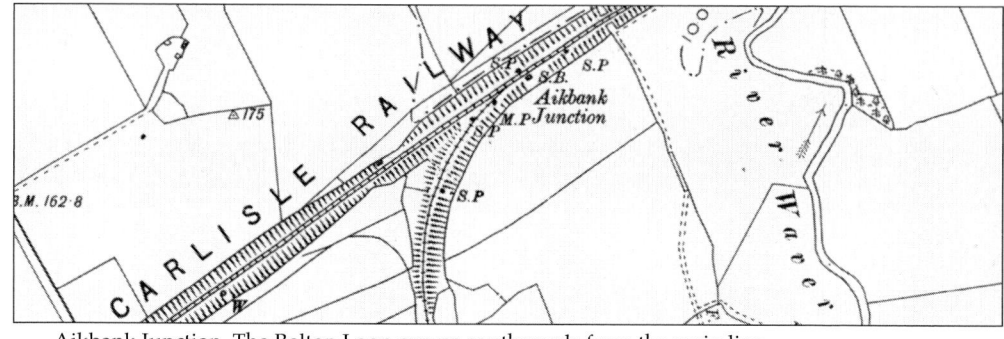

Aikbank Junction. The Bolton Loop curves southwards from the main line.
Reproduced from the 6in. Ordnance Survey map of 1899

Leegate station. *Reproduced from the 6in. Ordnance Survey map of 1899*

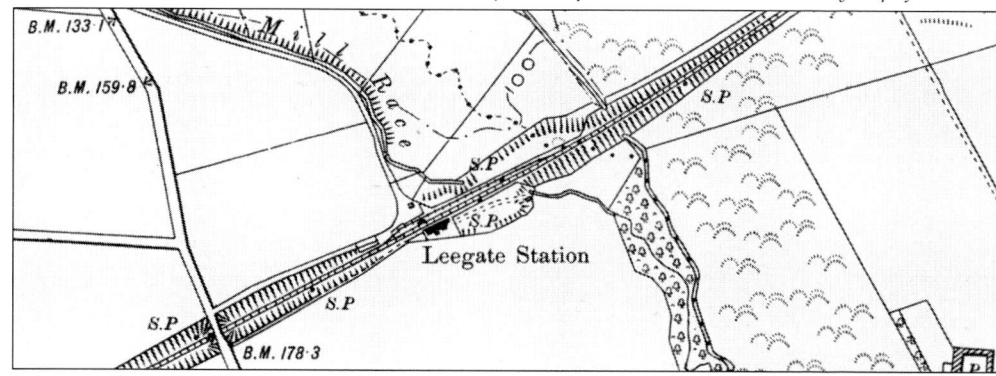

Leegate station in 1954, looking towards Carlisle. Passenger services had ceased on 5th June, 1950, but the station remained open to goods traffic until 2nd March, 1964.
W.A. Camwell/SLS Collection

Brayton Junction and its signal box viewed looking towards Carlisle, with the Kirtlebridge, Annan & Brayton Railway/Solway Junction Railway curving away to the left. *Richard Stenlake Collection*

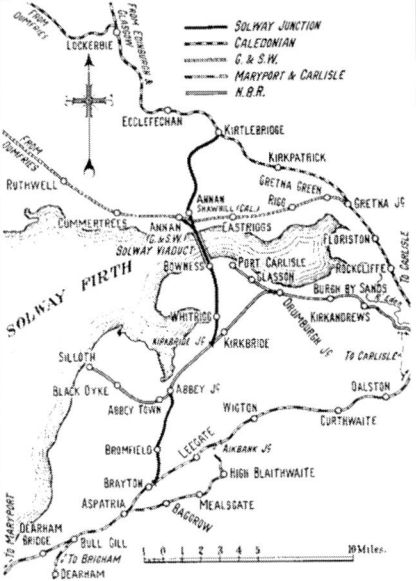

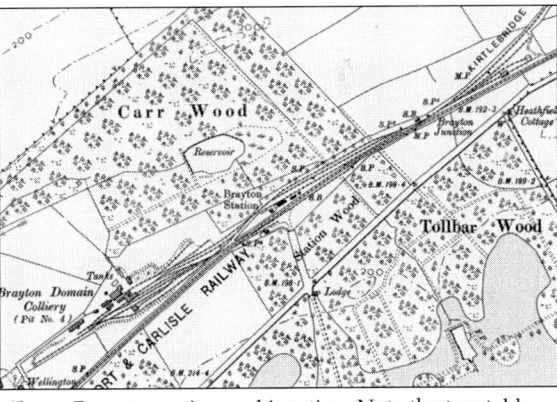

Above: Brayton station and junction. Note the turntable in the 'vee' of the junction.
Reproduced from the 6in. Ordnance Survey map of 1899

Left: Solway Junction Railway map, showing connecting routes from Brayton Junction to Scotland via the Solway Viaduct. The last train crossed the viaduct on 31st August, 1921.   *Railway Magazine*

Brayton station viewed towards Carlisle.   *John Alsop Collection*

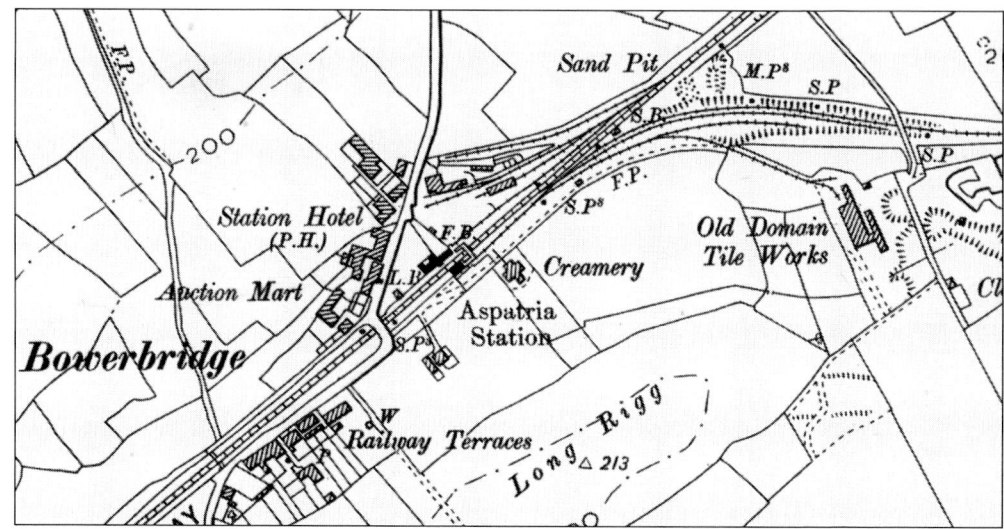

Aspatria station. The southern end of the Bolton Loop swings east, away from the main line.
Reproduced from the 6in. Ordnance Survey map of 1899

Seen from the down platform at Aspatria, this view shows the two lines as they diverge northwards. The original main line passes in front of the signal box in the distance before continuing beneath the road overbridge towards Wigton and Carlisle. The Bolton Loop veers off to the right. Note the double slip point just beyond the platform and a passenger train to the right of it which appears to be being shunted. *Author's Collection*

ALONG THE LINE IN THE LATE 19TH CENTURY

A commercial postcard view of the platform at Aspatria, looking towards Maryport.
Richard Stenlake Collection

Aspatria viewed from the western end of the down platform, showing the station building and footbridge beyond.
John Alsop Collection

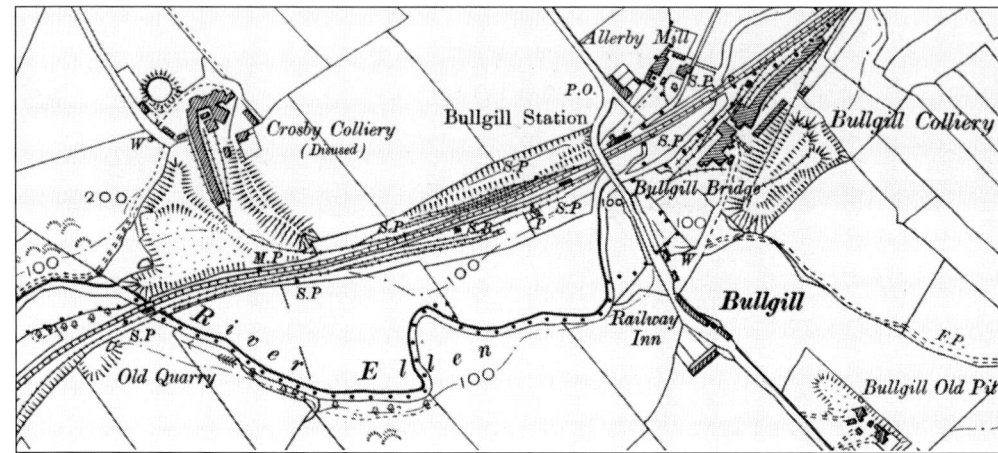

Bullgill station and surrounding collieries. The Derwent branch curves away south (*bottom left*).
Reproduced from the 6in. Ordnance Survey map of 1899

A train from Maryport enters Bullgill station. The platforms at Bullgill were staggered either side of a road overbridge, with the station building being on the up platform. The station nameboard reads 'Bullgill for Cockermouth'.
John Alsop Collection

West of the overbridge at Bullgill, the M&CR main line down platform face, for trains to Maryport, is on the left. A train stands in the Derwent branch bay platform. The group of dignitaries include John F. Gairns, editor of the *Railway Magazine* from 1911 to 1930, who is third left from the train.
John Alsop Collection

ALONG THE LINE IN THE LATE 19TH CENTURY

Dearham Bridge station looks well-maintained in this period postcard view, looking towards Carlisle. *Richard Stenlake Collection*

Dearham Bridge station and the rail link to Crosshow Colliery to the south.
Reproduced from the 6in. Ordnance Survey map of 1899

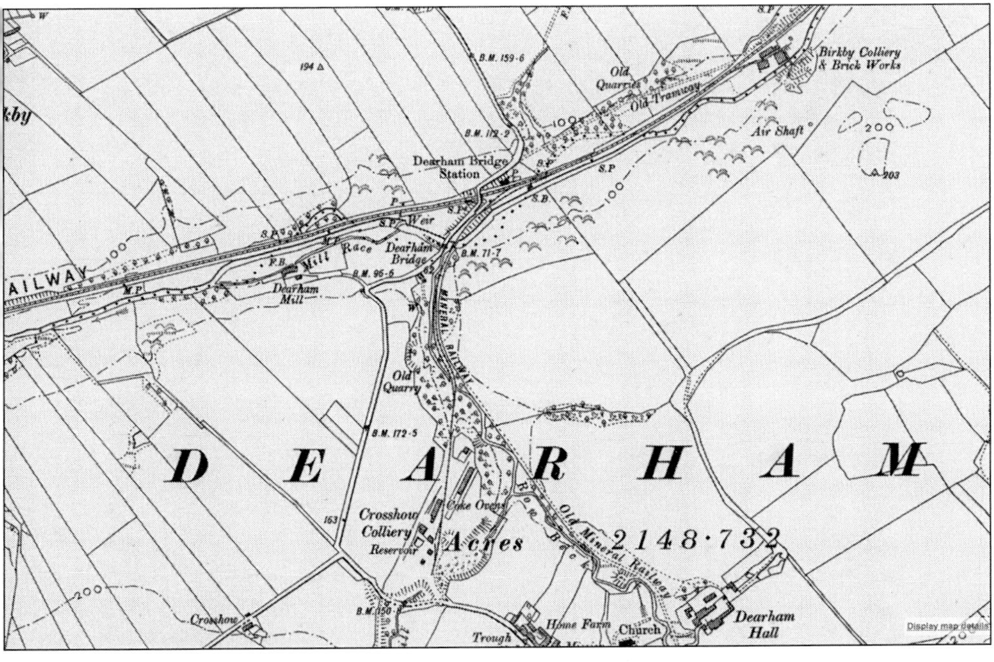

A view along Station Street at Maryport with the River Ellen bridge in the foreground. The impressive station buildings at Maryport provided the head office for the Maryport & Carlisle Railway. The station master's house is on the left.
John Alsop Collection

Maryport station and docks. The LNWR's line from Whitehaven formed an end-on junction with the Maryport & Carlisle just south of the goods station and the M&CR's branch into the docks. The Maryport & Carlisle Railway engine shed was sited between its junction into the docks and the River Ellen. Access into the docks for the LNWR was gained from Maryport Dock Junction (also known as Docks Branch Junction), immediately south of Solway Iron Works.
Reproduced from the 6in. Ordnance Survey map of 1899

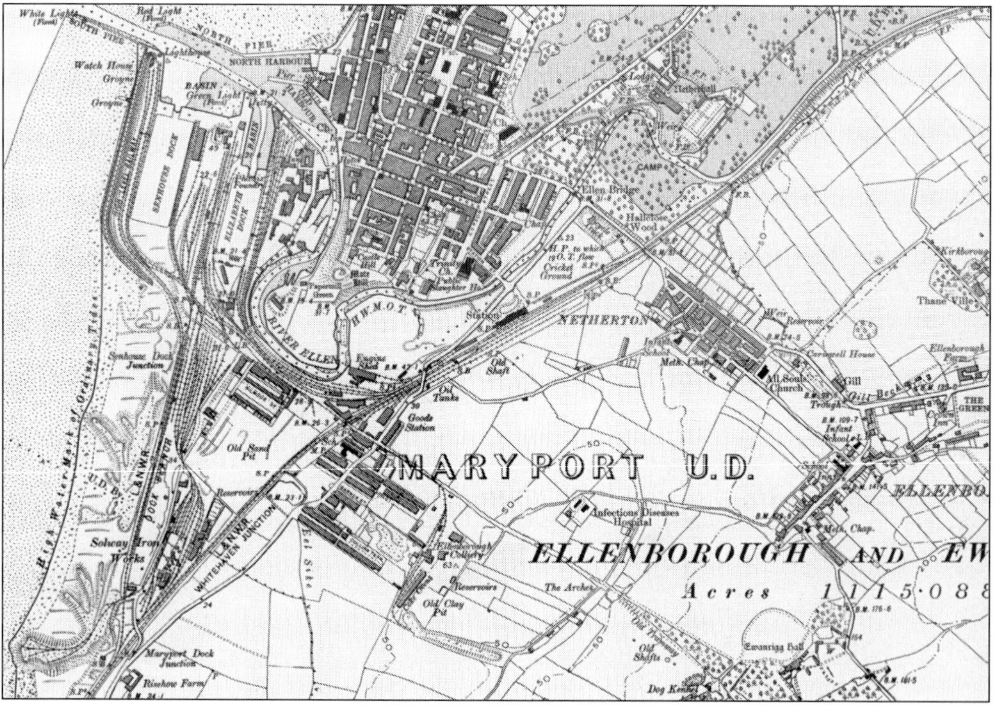

This pre-World War I view shows the imposing station building at Maryport. The up train waiting to depart is in the hands of 2-4-0 No. R1 and is made up of four-and six-wheel vehicles.
Author's Collection

This Valentine's series commercial postcard of Senhouse Dock, Maryport, shows a busy scene. A considerable number of sailing ships vie for berths alongside steam-powered vessels in this 1897 view published some years later. *Richard Stenlake Collection*

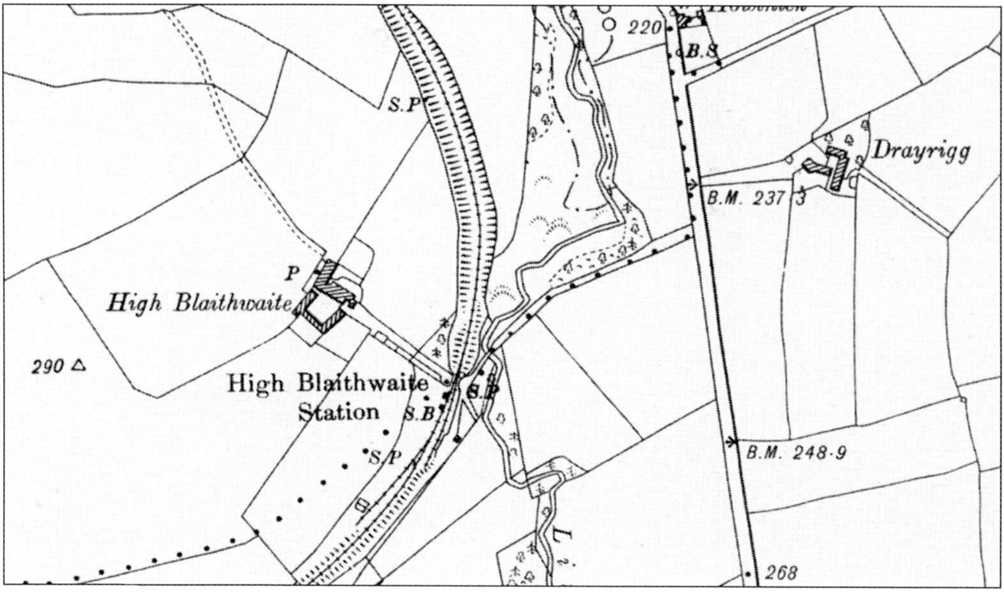

High Blaithwaite station.

Reproduced from the 6in. Ordnance Survey map of 1899

The modest station at High Blaithwaite was the first one on the Bolton Loop line reached by down trains. It opened later than the others on the loop, on 1st October, 1878, and it was also the first to be closed, on 1st August, 1921. The small cabin in the foreground houses a ground frame.

John Alsop Collection

ALONG THE LINE IN THE LATE 19TH CENTURY

The Bolton Loop

The junctions for the 'Bolton Loop' are seen when making the journey along the main line. This additional section, the first extension to be built by the company, at the northerly end leaves the main line at Aikbank, effectively swinging southwards in a wide arc before linking back onto the main line.

The first station on this section is High Blaithwaite and after this is Mealsbank. The stations on this section serve small communities and also the sawmills in this area. Travelling further south is Allhallows Colliery, a substantial operation and clearly an asset as far as the railway is concerned. The only other station on this off-shoot is Baggrow. Further south is Brayton Domain Colliery, another substantial enterprise, just before the branch meets up with the main line again. The loop is just over seven miles long.

Staff pose for the photographer in this view of Mealsgate station. Passenger trains north of here ceased from 1st August, 1921, but a passenger service continued to Aspatria until 22nd September, 1930. *John Alsop Collection*

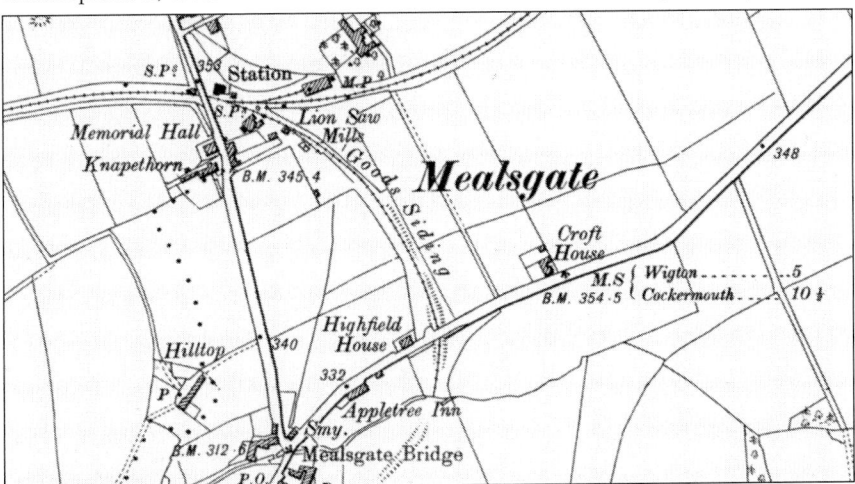

Mealsgate station and goods siding. *Reproduced from the 6in. Ordnance Survey map of 1899*

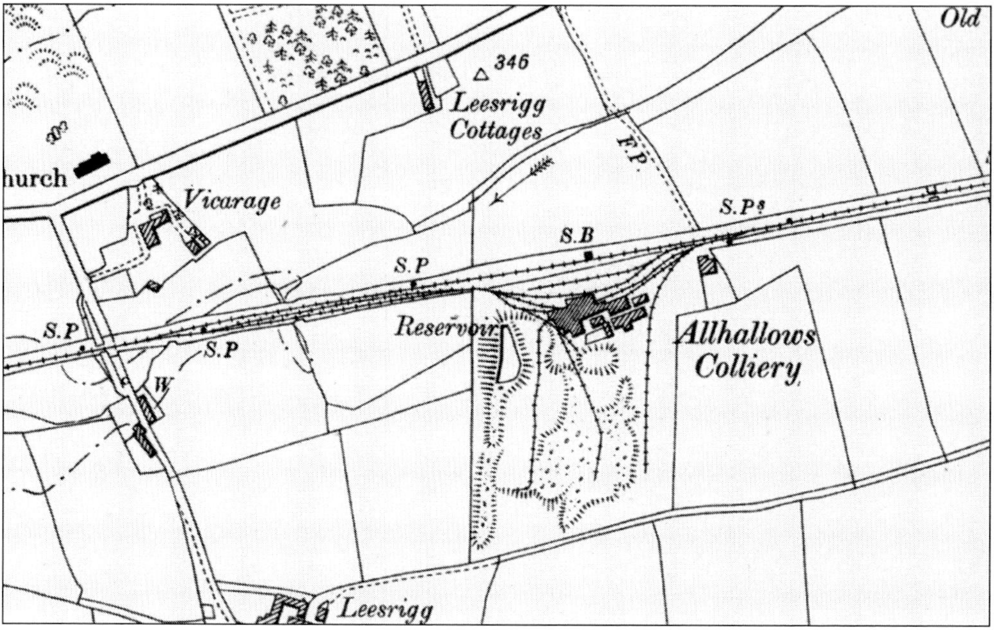

Allhallows Colliery. *Reproduced from the 6in. Ordnance Survey map of 1899*

Baggrow station. *Reproduced from the 6in. Ordnance Survey map of 1899*

A porter poses for the photographer beneath Baggrow's station clock. *John Alsop Collection*

Brayton Domain Colliery. *Reproduced from the 6in. Ordnance Survey map of 1899*

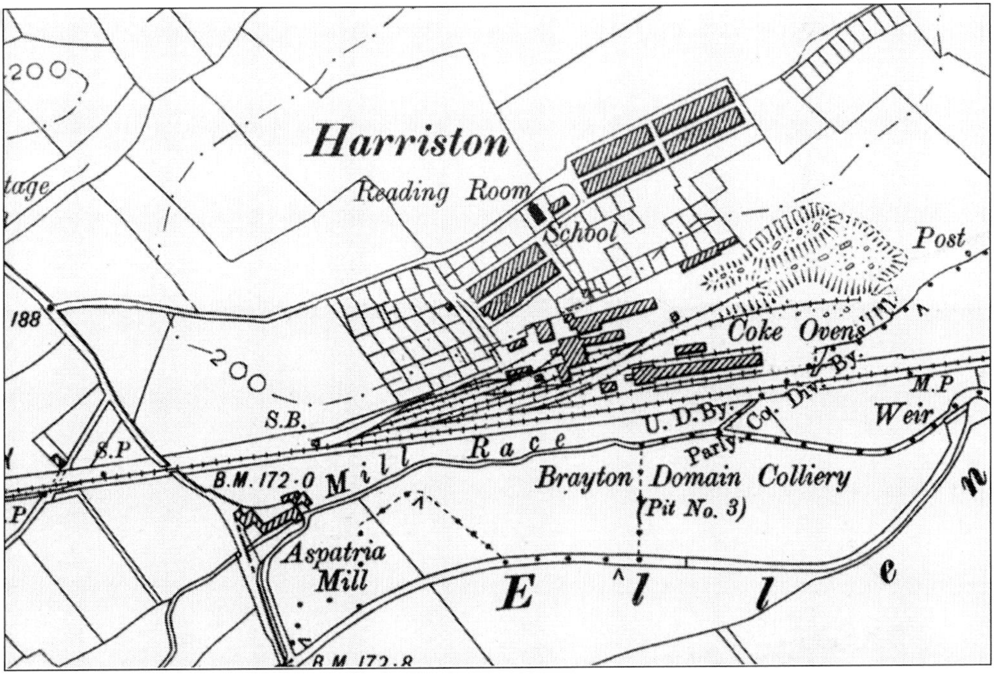

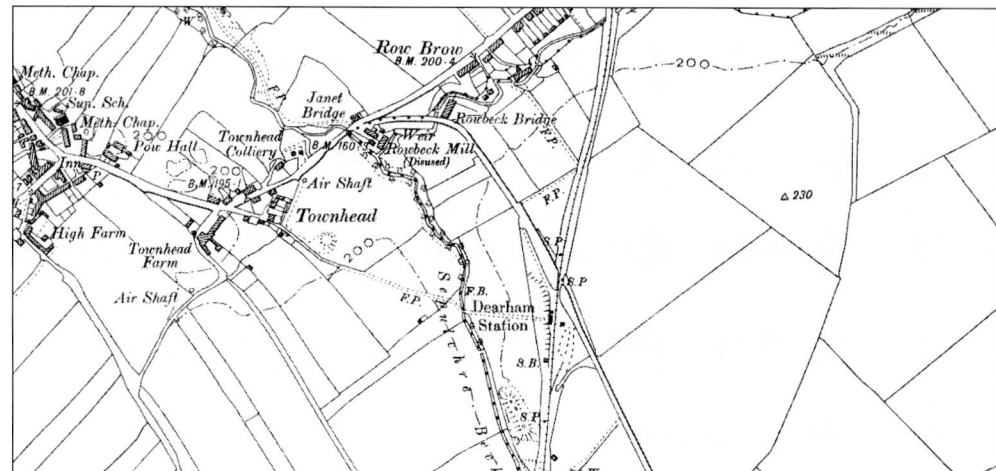

Dearham station was the longest-lived of the passenger stations on the Derwent branch, surviving until 29th April, 1935 and the end of passenger services on the line.

Reproduced from the 6in. Ordnance Survey map of 1899

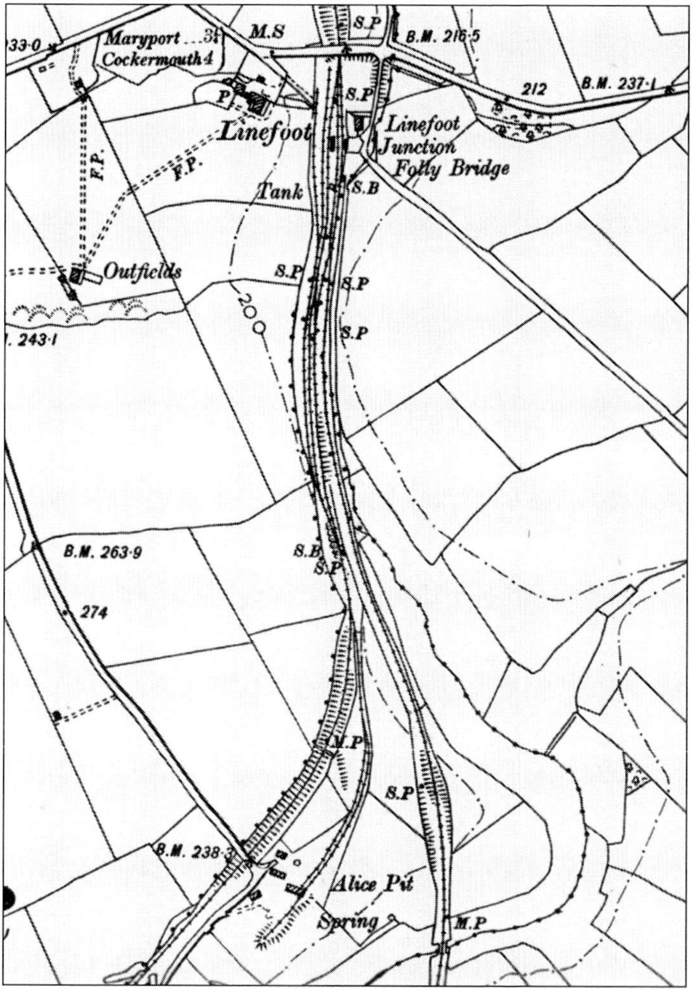

Linefoot station and junction. The Cleator & Workington Junction Railway line to Workington veers away to the south-west, while the Derwent branch takes a more southerly route. The line to Alice Pit is situated within the 'vee' of the diverging lines.

Reproduced from the 6in. Ordnance Survey map of 1899

ALONG THE LINE IN THE LATE 19TH CENTURY

The Derwent Branch

The last section of the railway to have been built leaves the main line just south of Bullgill station. It runs almost southwards through a mainly rural setting with open countryside. The first station on the line is Dearham and after Dovenby Close it reaches Linefoot where there is a junction with the Cleator & Workington Junction Railway.

The line then runs in a wide arc in an easterly direction. On this section is Dovenby Lodge station which is a private station. The fact that after this arc the line swings southward suggests what could well be seen as a deviation of the line simply to enable this private station. The station has all the elements usually found in railway stations used by the general public. There is a ticket office complete with a clerk, and also a waiting room. The owner of Dovenby Hall, Mrs Ballantine Dykes, well-connected with the coming of this railway, clearly felt the need to impress her guests.

The next station, Papcastle, is the penultimate station on the line. This place, like others in this area, had a Roman settlement and was known as Derventio. After this station there is a junction with what was part of the London & North Western Railway, this is Brigham station.

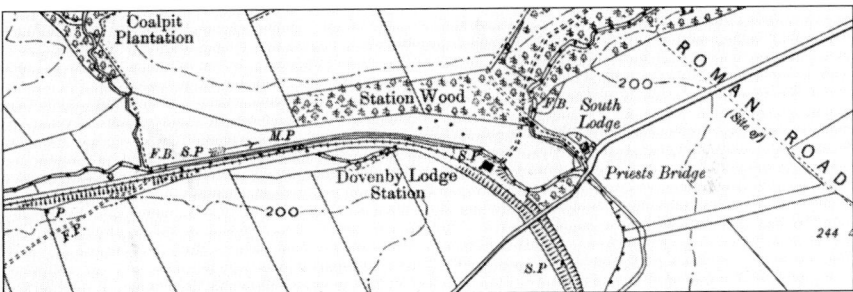

Dovenby Lodge station.
Reproduced from the 6in. Ordnance Survey map of 1899

A 1970 view of Dovenby Lodge private station. The station building was built of local coarse stone with ashlar facings in a Tudor style.
G. Biddle/ Kidderminster Railway Museum.

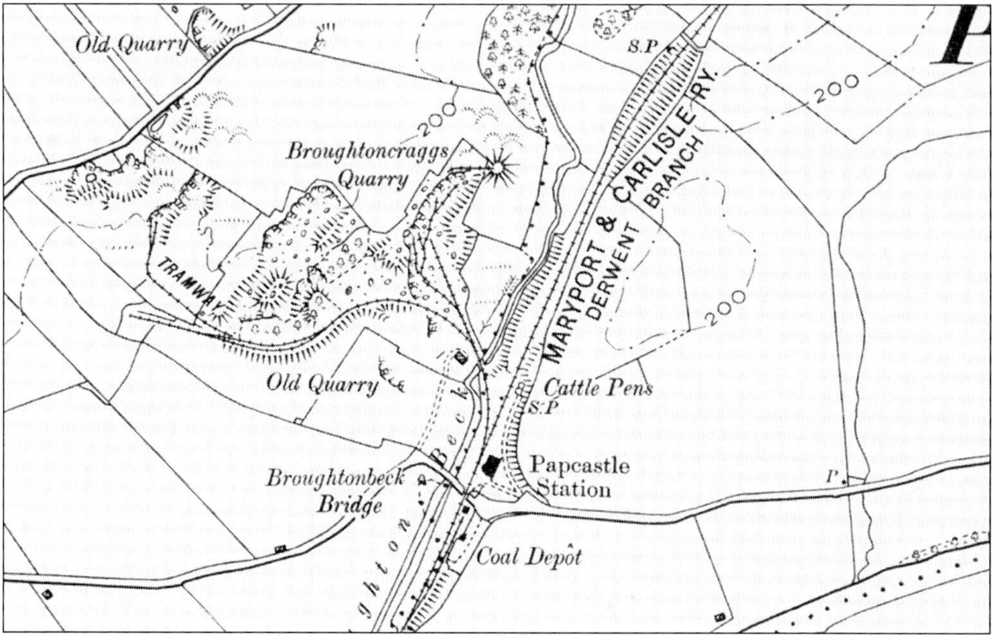

Papcastle station and adjacent quarries.   *Reproduced from the 6in. Ordnance Survey map of 1899*

The substantial station building at Papcastle in May 1966, it had closed almost 45 years earlier on 1st July, 1921.   *John Alsop*

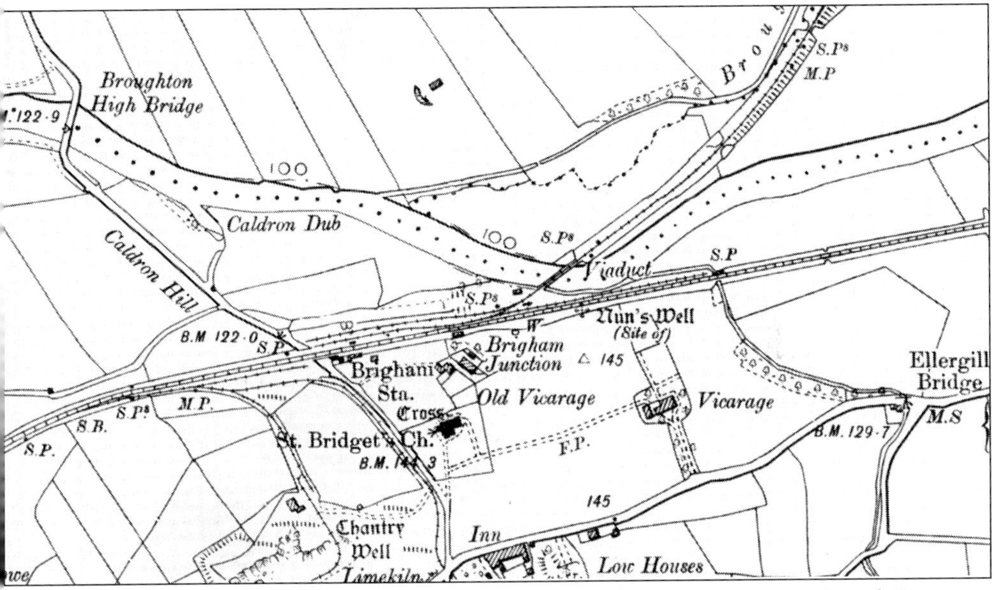

ALONG THE LINE IN THE LATE 19TH CENTURY

The London & North Western Railway station at Brigham. The M&CR's Derwent branch forms a junction with the LNWR's Workington-Cockermouth just east of the station having crossed the River Derwent on a viaduct.   *Reproduced from the 6in. Ordnance Survey map of 1899*

The level crossing at Brigham, with the station to the left and signal box to the right. St Bridget's Church is in the distance. Brigham station was closed, with the former LNWR line, on 18th April, 1966.   *John Alsop Collection*

Chapter Eight

Locomotives and rolling stock

The first locomotives ordered by the Maryport & Carlisle Railway could hardly have been sourced more locally. The railway placed orders for two engines with Tulk & Ley & Co. of Lowca, situated some 10 miles south of Maryport along the Cumbrian coast. Perhaps it was a bold decision to place the order in 1840 with the iron foundry in Lowca, as engines Nos. 1 and 2 were the first locomotives that Tulk & Ley had ever built. Despite Lowca being not too many miles away, the difficulty of transporting these locomotives overland led to them being moved by sea on rafts. No. 1 *Ellen*, a 2-2-2, arrived in January 1840 with 0-6-0 No. 2 *Brayton* arriving the following month. No. 1 was supplied at a cost of £1,580, and No. 2 £1,720. Clearly the railway was satisfied with the Tulk & Ley products as the Lowca-based manufacturer was to supply a further five locomotives to the Maryport & Carlisle, the last being ordered in 1854. By 1857 Tulk & Ley had been taken over by Fletcher Jennings & Co.

The known details of the first two locomotives are:

Locomotive	*No. 1 Ellen**	*No. 2 Brayton†*
Type	2-2-2	0-6-0
Driving wheel diameter	5ft 0in.	4ft 6in
Cylinders	12in. x 18 in.	14in. x 18in.

* Scrapped by 1850. † Rebuilt in 1854 as an 0-4-2.

For the next locomotive, 0-6-0 No. 3 *Ballantine Dykes*, the Maryport & Carlisle turned to R. & W. Hawthorn Ltd in Newcastle. The company was formed by brothers Robert and William Hawthorn in 1820 and their experience with railway locomotives had a rather longer history than Tulk & Ley. The brothers had been in attendance at the Liverpool & Manchester Railway's Rainhill Trials in 1829 and by the 1830s they had supplied locomotives to the Stockton & Darlington, Newcastle & Carlisle and Great Western railways. Delivered in 1842, No. 3 was rebuilt in 1858. Known dimensions are:

Locomotive	*No. 3 Ballantine Dykes*
Type	0-6-0
Driving wheel diameter	4ft 6in
Cylinders	14in. x 18in.

The Maryport & Carlisle returned to Tulk & Ley when ordering 2-2-2 No. 4 *Harrison*, delivered in March 1843. Known details for this locomotive are:

Locomotive	*No. 4 Harrison*
Type	2-2-2
Driving wheel diameter	5ft 6in.
Cylinders	13in. x 18 in.

LOCOMOTIVES AND ROLLING STOCK

R. & W. Hawthorn Ltd won the orders for the next two locomotives, 0-6-0 No. 5 *Sir Wilfrid* in 1843, and 0-4-2 No. 6 *Senhouse* in 1845. *Senhouse* underwent a rebuild in 1853. Known details of these locomotives are:

Locomotive	No. 5 *Sir Wilfrid*	No. 6 *Senhouse*
Type	0-6-0	0-4-2
Driving wheel diameter	4ft 6in.	5ft 0in.
Cylinders	14in. x 18in.	14in. x 21in.

The Maryport & Carlisle returned to Tulk & Ley for its next three locomotives, all 0-4-2s. No. 7 *Lowca*, and No. 8 *Harris* were built in 1845, and subsequently rebuilt in 1855 and 1852 respectively. No. 9 arrived in 1847; it is unclear whether this locomotive ever carried a name, but was possiblely called *Cocker*. Known details of these locomotives are:

Locomotives	No. 7 *Lowca*, No. 8 *Harris* and No. 9
Type	0-4-2
Driving wheel diameter	4ft 9in.
Cylinders	14in. x 21in.

Another 0-6-0 from R. & W. Hawthorn Ltd was next to arrive. No. 10 *Derwent* was delivered in 1848. This locomotive was subsequently rebuilt in 1854, and its known dimensions are:

Locomotives	No. 10 *Derwent*
Type	0-6-0
Driving wheel diameter	4ft 6in.
Cylinders	15in. x 24in.

Thomas Richardson & Sons of Hartlepool were awarded the next locomotive order. Richardson's earliest locomotives dated back to 1840 when it supplied four engines to the Hartlepool Railway. The 1850 order from the Maryport & Carlisle arrived when Richardsons were busy supplying locomotives to the York, Newcastle & Berwick Railway. The new locomotive was another 0-6-0, and was to be the only Richardson engine in the Maryport & Carlisle stock list. No. 11 was un-named, it was rebuilt in 1856 and withdrawn in 1868. No. 11's known dimensions are:

Locomotive	No. 11
Type	0-6-0
Driving wheel diameter	5ft 0in.
Cylinders	15in. x 22in.

No. 12 was the final engine ordered by the Maryport & Carlisle from Tulk & Ley and was quite unlike the products that had preceded it. The locomotive was a 4-2-0 built under the patent of Thomas Russell Crampton *(illustrated on the cover)*. Tulk & Ley's place in locomotive history is assured as the first to build a Crampton locomotive. The general principle of the Crampton design was that the driving wheel was placed behind the locomotive's firebox. This allowed the boiler to be pitched lower, thus giving a lower centre of gravity. At that period

The C. Hamilton Ellis original print of Crampton locomotive No. 12. *Author's Collection*

there were concerns about the centre of gravity and the risk of locomotives overturning at speed. The Crampton patent offered a solution to this. Because the size of the driving wheels was not governed by the pitch of the boiler a larger driving wheel diameter could be used. With the axle of the driving wheel behind the firebox, No. 12 was able to employ a driving wheel of some 7ft in diameter, with 16in. x 20in. outside cylinders.

Tulk & Ley's first three Crampton locomotives were built for the Namur & Liege Railway in Belgium. The order was placed in 1845, and the engines were completed the following year. On completion, the Namur & Liege was unable to take delivery, so the locomotives were acquired by the South Eastern Railway. A further four Cramptons were built by Tulk & Ley in 1847 and 1848, with the final locomotive of this type built at Lowca being the Maryport & Carlisle's No. 12 in 1854.

Around 300 Crampton locomotives were built in Europe, 51 of these in Great Britain. The type enjoyed significantly more success on the Continent, particularly in France and Germany. The large driving wheel could give greater speed. However, with the driving wheel behind the firebox there was insufficient adhesive weight available. This could make starting trains very difficult. As a result, the Cramptons tended to be used on lightly-loaded trains where traction was less of an issue and, once moving, they could show off their speed. Quite how well No. 12 coped with the often damp conditions that prevail in Cumbria is a matter of conjecture! The issue of poor traction saw many Cramptons rebuilt in order to resolve the problem. No. 12 was rebuilt as a 2-2-2 in 1860, and in that form gave a further 10 years service to the Maryport & Carlisle. The locomotive captured the imagination of renowned railway writer and painter C. Hamilton Ellis (1909-1987) and his depiction of No. 12 is reproduced on the front cover and above. An example of a Crampton locomotive survives in preservation, in the Cité du Train (the French National Railway Museum) at Mulhouse.

No. 13 was sole example of an E.B. Wilson locomotive on the Maryport & Carlisle Railway. Built in Leeds in 1855, this 0-6-0 had 4ft 9in driving wheels with 15in. x 22in. cylinders. It was to remain in service until 1874.

The first of two Manchester-built Sharp, Stewart locomotives to be delivered to the Maryport & Carlisle was No. 14 of 1855. It was an 0-6-0 with 5ft 0in. driving wheels with 15in. x 28in. cylinders. It was rebuilt in 1868, and in rebuilt form gave a further 11 years service. No. 14 passed to the duplicate list in 1877 and was renumbered R1.

LOCOMOTIVES AND ROLLING STOCK

With George Tosh now in charge as Locomotive Superintendent, the decision was made to build the next locomotive, No. 5, in the railway's own workshops at Maryport. It was to be the first of 33 locomotives built here over a period of 43 years, although the railway did continue to order from outside locomotive builders. No. 5 was also significant as it was the last locomotive on the Maryport & Carlisle built to the 2-2-2 wheel arrangement and the first Maryport locomotive to use an engine number that had become available due to an earlier withdrawal. This was a practice that became commonplace from this date forwards, leading to locomotives of the same type not having consecutive numbers, with the sole exception of the railway's final locomotives, the Yorkshire Engine Co. class '29' which was delivered in 1921. No. 5 remained in service until 1872, and its known dimensions are:

Locomotive	*No. 5*
Type	2-2-2
Driving wheel diameter	6ft 0in.
Cylinders	14in. x 22in.

The next locomotive to arrive on the railway was the Manchester product, Sharp, Stewart & Co.-built No. 15, an 0-4-2. Built in 1859, it was rebuilt in 1869, and then served until 1884. This engine had 5ft 6in. driving wheels and 15in. x 24in. cylinders. It was moved to the duplicate list and renumbered as R1 in 1880. The R1 number had become available as the previous incumbent, originally No. 14 of 1855, had been withdrawn in 1877.

Having built 2-2-2 No. 5 at Maryport in 1857, locomotive production got into full swing from 1859. In the next 12 years all the railway's locomotive requirements were satisfied by the works in Maryport, some 16 engines in all. The first of these was 0-4-0 No. 9. The locomotive had 15in. x 22in. cylinders, and in 1869 it was rebuilt, giving a further six years service, withdrawal finally coming in 1875.

The next three locomotives built at Maryport were 0-4-2s. No. 6 was built in 1860, with Nos. 8 and 10 following in 1863. All three had 15in. x 22in. cylinders. Nos. 6 and 10 had driving wheels of 5ft 6in. diameter, while No. 8 had larger, 6ft 0in., wheels. No. 10 was placed on the duplicate list as No. R2 in 1878; it was then rebuilt in 1880, and was to survive until 1897.

A broadside view of 0-4-2 No. 8 of 1863.   *John Alsop Collection*

The Maryport-built 0-4-2T No. 17 of 1865. *Author's Collection*

No. 17 was a long-lived locomotive. In 1907 the 0-4-2T was rebuilt as an 0-6-0T, as seen here. In this later form the engine continued into LMS days, as No. 11563, before eventual withdrawal in 1927. Note the engine retains its secondary buffers for use with chaldron wagons.

John Alsop Collection

LOCOMOTIVES AND ROLLING STOCK

It is perhaps a little surprising that up to this point in Maryport & Carlisle locomotive history there had been no tank engines on the railway. This was to change with the building of the next two locomotives at Maryport, 0-4-2 saddle tanks. In 1864 No. 4 entered service, with No. 7 being constructed the following year. No. 7 was renumbered as R3 when being moved to the duplicate list in 1882. It carried the R3 identity for some 10 years before being withdrawn. Comparative dimensions for these 0-4-2STs are:

Locomotive	No. 4	No. 7
Type	0-4-2ST	0-4-2ST
Driving wheel diameter	4ft 9in.	4ft 6in
Cylinders	15in. x 22in.	14½in. x 22in.

Another product from the works in Maryport during 1865 was 0-6-0 No. 16. This locomotive had 4ft 6in. driving wheels and 16in. x 22in. cylinders. It was rebuilt in 1873, with withdrawal coming in 1895.

An 0-4-2 side tank, No. 17, was built at Maryport in 1865. It had 4ft 9in. driving wheels and 15in. x 22in. cylinders, with Stephenson inside valve gear. The locomotive continued in this form until 1907 when it was rebuilt as an 0-6-0T (*see facing page*). The engine remained in service until 1927, being allocated the LMS number 11563 at the 1923 Grouping. Details of the locomotive in rebuilt form were:

LMS No.	11563
Type	0-6-0T
Driving wheel diameter	4ft 9½in.
Cylinders	17in. x 24in.
Boiler pressure	140lb.
Tractive effort	15,150lb.
LMS power classification	1F
Weight	35 tons 10 cwt

The works at Maryport built a single engine in 1866, 0-6-0 No. 1 which had 5ft 0in. driving wheels and 15¾in. x 24in. cylinders. This locomotive was rebuilt in 1888. In 1900 the engine was transferred to the duplicate list being allocated the number R4 and it was rebuilt again in 1903. This long-lived engine survived into LMS days, becoming No. 12077, it was withdrawn in August 1924.

The year 1867 saw two locomotives built at Maryport. The first of these was 0-4-2T No. 18 which had 5ft 2in. driving wheels and 15in. x 22in. cylinders. In 1908 the locomotive was transferred to the duplicate list, becoming No. R5. Withdrawal came in 1923.

The other product of 1867 was a 2-4-0 type, the Maryport & Carlisle's first of this wheel arrangement. No. 19 had 6ft 0in. driving wheels and 15in. x 22in. cylinders. It was transferred to the duplicate list in 1884 as No. R1 and it survived until 1921.

The only locomotive built at Maryport in 1868 was 0-6-0 No. 11. It had 5ft 0in. driving wheels and 15¾in. x 24in. cylinders. No. 11 became No. R3 on the duplicate list in 1881 and it was withdrawn the following year. Another 0-6-0, No. 2 was constructed in 1869, and this engine remained in service until 1886.

Maryport-built 0-6-0 No. 1 of 1866 was rebuilt in 1888, and a further rebuild came in 1903. Ultimately it gave 68 years of service, before being withdrawn by the LMS in 1924.

John Alsop Collection

A view showing 0-4-2T No. 18 of 1867 coupled to a brake van. It was another long-lived engine, withdrawal coming in 1923.

John Alsop Collection

LOCOMOTIVES AND ROLLING STOCK

M&CR 0-6-0 No. 12, originally built in 1870. *John Alsop Collection*

No. 12, built at Maryport in 1870, was another 0-6-0 to survive into LMS days. This locomotive had 5ft 1in. driving wheels and 17in. x 24in. cylinders. It was first rebuilt in 1883, and then again in 1901. It was allocated the LMS number 12078, and was not withdrawn until 1924.

In 1870 George Tosh was succeeded as Locomotive Superintendent by Hugh Smellie who had previously worked under the Stirling brothers on the Glasgow & South Western Railway in Kilmarnock. His tenure on the Maryport & Carlisle was to last until 1878. He then returned to Kilmarnock to become Locomotive Superintendent of the Glasgow & South Western Railway until 1890.

Two locomotives of class '6', 0-6-0s Nos. 6 and 20, were built during 1871. The class '6' engines had 5ft 1½in. driving wheels and 17in. x 24in. cylinders. Both survived into LMS days, to 1928 and 1929 respectively. No. 6 underwent rebuilds in 1880, 1895 and 1907, while No. 20's rebuilds came in 1881, 1906 and 1921.

Three rebuilds for 1871-built 0-6-0 No. 20, enabled this locomotive to give 58 years of service. It was withdrawn by the LMS in 1929. *John Alsop Collection*

Beyer, Peacock-built 0-6-0 No. 21. *Author's Collection*

M&CR 0-4-2 No. 23 of 1872 was another Beyer, Peacock product, seen here with its domeless boiler. *Author's Collection*

LOCOMOTIVES AND ROLLING STOCK

Having been self-sufficient for its locomotives since 1859, the railway then turned to Beyer, Peacock in Manchester for its next engines, three 0-6-0s and an 0-4-2. The 0-6-0s of class '21' carried the numbers 21, 22 and 24. These engines had 4ft 8½in. driving wheels with 17in. x 24in. cylinders. The first to be rebuilt was No. 22 in 1897, with Nos. 24 and 21 following in 1899 and 1903 respectively. No. 22 was scrapped in 1923, with Nos. 21 and 24 lasting until 1924 and 1925 having been allocated LMS numbers 12081 and 12082. Details of former Maryport 0-6-0s allocated LMS Nos. 12077 to 12082 are as follows:

LMS Nos.	12077-12080	12081-12082
Type	0-6-0	0-6-0
Driving wheel diameter	5ft 1½in.	4ft 9in.
Cylinders	17in. x 24in.	17in. x 24in.
Valve gear	Stephenson	Stephenson
Boiler pressure	140lb.	140lb.
Tractive effort	13,400lb.	14,600lb.
LMS power classification	1F	1F
Weight	33 tons 5 cwt	33 tons 5 cwt

The Maryport & Carlisle acquired an 0-4-2 from Beyer, Peacock in 1872. This was No. 23 which had 4ft 8½in. driving wheels with 16in. x 24in. cylinders. The locomotive was rebuilt in 1891, and was sold out of service in 1923.

Maryport Works built two 0-4-2s in 1873, Nos. 3 and 5. No. 3 was rebuilt twice, in 1886 and 1904, and was withdrawn in 1923 without being allocated an LMS number. No. 5's rebuilds came in 1884 and 1903, with this engine succumbing a little earlier, in 1921. These locomotives had driving wheels of 5ft 7½in. diameter and 16in. x 22in. cylinders.

Maryport-built 0-4-2 No. 3 gave 50 years of service. *John Alsop Collection*

2-4-0 No. 8 was a long-lived engine, almost reaching its half century. Originally built in 1876, it survived into LMS days, having been rebuilt in 1895. *John Alsop Collection*

0-6-0 No. 9 at Carlisle Currock shed. An M&CR open wagon is servicing the coaling stage in the background. *John Alsop Collection*

LOCOMOTIVES AND ROLLING STOCK

The first of Hugh Smellie's class '13' 2-4-0s was introduced in 1873, the eponymous No. 13. Two other members of the class followed, No. 8 in 1876 and No. 10 two years later. All three survived beyond the Grouping, having been allocated LMS numbers 10005-10007 (for Nos. 13, 8 and 10 respectively). No. 13 was rebuilt three times, in 1887, 1894 and 1905, while No. 8 was rebuilt just once (1895) and No. 10 underwent rebuilds in 1898 and 1910. No. 13 was the first of the class to be withdrawn, in 1924; its sister engines were to follow in 1925. Details of the '13' class in their final form are:

LMS Nos.	10005-10007
Type	2-4-0
Driving wheel diameter	6ft 1½in.
Cylinders	17in. x 24in.
Valve gear	Stephenson
Boiler pressure	135lb.
Tractive effort	10,828lb.
Weight	33 tons 2 cwt

The first of the class '9' 0-6-0s was built in 1875. The two members of this class No. 9 and 14 (of 1877) were long-lived, not being withdrawn until 1930. No. 9 went through rebuilds in 1883, 1898 and 1922, while No. 14 had its only rebuild in 1887. No. 9 became 12484 at Grouping, while No. 14 was renumbered 12485.

The next locomotive acquisition on the railway was the first of three 0-6-0s from Beyer, Peacock of class '25'. No. 25 arrived in 1878. There was a considerable delay before it was joined by sister engines, No. 27 in 1890, and No. 28 in 1899. All three engines would receive one rebuild, in 1899, 1900 and 1922 respectively. Nos. 25, 27 and 28 became LMS Nos. 12486, 12490 and 12491. The first to be withdrawn was No. 12490 (ex-27), with the other two following in 1930.

The next new type to be built at Maryport was the class '4' 0-4-2s, with No. 4 constructed in 1879, followed by No. 15 in 1892 and No. 16 in 1895. There were rebuilds for No. 4 in 1889 and 1904. Rebuilds for Nos. 15 and 16 came considerably later, in 1916 and 1920 respectively. All of these locomotives

Beyer, Peacock-built 0-6-0 No. 25. *John Alsop Collection*

M&CR 0-4-0T No. R2, formerly No. 26, was one of two distinctive looking Neilson-built tank locomotives which were used on shunting duties at Maryport docks. *Author's Collection*

M&CR 0-6-0 No. 11. The locomotive underwent two rebuilds, in 1891 and 1902.
Author's Collection

LOCOMOTIVES AND ROLLING STOCK

passed to the LMS at the 1923 Grouping, when Nos. 4, 15 and 16 became 10010, 10012 and 10013 respectively. These locomotives were withdrawn in 1928. Details of the class '4' locomotives in their final form are:

LMS Nos.	**10010, 10012, 10013**
Type	0-4-2
Driving wheel diameter	5ft 7½in.
Cylinders	17in. x 24in.
Valve gear	Stephenson
Boiler pressure	150lb.
Tractive effort	13,100lb.
LMS power classification	1P
Weight	33 tons 10 cwt

In 1880 and 1881 the railway took receipt of two side tanks from Neilson & Co. of Glasgow. Nos. 15 and 26 were unusual looking machines used on shunting duties in Maryport docks. They had driving wheels of just 3ft 8in., with 14in. x 20in. cylinders. Both were placed on the duplicate list, No. 15 in 1880 became R3, and sister engine No. 26 was renumbered R2 in 1897. Both passed to the LMS where they were allocated, but did not carry, the numbers 11259 and 11260. Withdrawal came in 1924.

The first of the class '11' 0-6-0s was built in Maryport in 1881, followed by No. 7 (1882), No. 19 (1884) and No. 1 (1900). No. 1 had the distinction of being the last new locomotive to be built at Maryport Works. No. 11 was subsequently rebuilt in 1891, and then again in 1902, while No. 7's rebuilds were in 1903 and 1921. No. 19's rebuilds were later still – 1905 and 1922, while No. 1 was rebuilt in 1919. All these engines passed to the LMS when they were allocated LMS numbers 12487 (11), 12488 (7), 12489 (19) and 12492 (1). No. 11 was first to be withdrawn, in 1928, the other three members of the class were scrapped in 1930.

Maryport Works built 0-4-2 No. 2 in 1889. Having been rebuilt in 1903, it continued until 1928, by then having acquired the LMS number 10011. Details of No. 10011 in its final form are:

LMS No.	*10011*
Type	0-4-2
Driving wheel diameter	5ft 7½in.
Cylinders	17in. x 24in.
Valve gear	Stephenson
Boiler pressure	140lb.
Tractive effort	11,800lb.
LMS power classification	1P
Weight	32 tons

In 1897, with William Robinson as Locomotive Superintendent, a new type to the railway was introduced, an 0-4-4T. No. 26 was a very attractive well tank built for use on passenger services on the Derwent branch. Its driving wheels were of 5ft 1½in. diameter and it had 16in. x 22in. cylinders. The locomotive passed to the LMS, where it was allocated the number 10618 (although this number was never carried).

Maryport-built 0-4-2 No. 2 of 1889. *John Alsop Collection*

The attractive livery and clean lines of 0-4-4T No. 26 are on show in this view taken at Maryport engine shed. This locomotive was built at Maryport in 1897 specifically to work passenger trains on the Derwent branch. The engine survived into LMS days, who allocated it the number 10618, withdrawal came in 1925. *John Alsop Collection*

LOCOMOTIVES AND ROLLING STOCK

In the final 20 years of the Maryport & Carlisle only three new engines entered service, all were 0-6-0s. First came 0-6-0 No. 18 ordered from the North British Locomotive Co. in Glasgow. This company had been formed in 1903 with the amalgamation of Sharp, Stewart & Co., Neilson, Reid & Co. and Dübs & Co. thus becoming the largest locomotive manufacturer in Europe. No. 18 remained in original form until 1919 when it was rebuilt. It continued in service until 1925 with the LMS allocating it the number 12493. In 1923 the LMS grouped the ten members of Maryport & Carlisle classes '9', '11', '18', '25' under the single category of '2F'. The oldest of the '2Fs' was No. 9, of 1875 vintage, with No. 18 the newest. The ten ex-Maryport & Carlisle '2Fs' were:

LMS No.	M&C No.	M&C class	Builder	Built	Rebuilt	Withdrawn
12484	9	9	Maryport	1875	1883, 1898, 1922	1930
12485	14	9	Maryport	1877	1887	1925
12486	25	25	Beyer, Peacock	1878	1899	1930
12487	11	11	Maryport	1881	1891, 1902	1928
12488	7	11	Maryport	1882	1902, 1921	1930
12489	19	11	Maryport	1884	1905, 1922	1930
12490	27	25	Beyer, Peacock	1890	1900	1928
12491	28	25	Beyer, Peacock	1899	1922	1930
12492	1	11	Maryport	1900	1919	1930
12493	18	18	North British Loco. Co.	1908	1919	1925

Variations amongst the '2Fs' meant that locomotive weights were between 36 tons 5 cwt and 39 tons 15 cwt. Details of the '2Fs' in their final form are:

LMS Nos.	12484 & 12485	12486-93
Type	0-6-0	0-6-0
Driving wheel diameter	5ft 1½in.	5ft 1½in.
Cylinders	18in. x 28in.	18in. x 26in.
Valve gear	Stephenson	Stephenson
Boiler pressure	140lb.	140lb.
Tractive effort	17,550lb.	16,300lb.

The Maryport & Carlisle Railway's final Locomotive Superintendent, John Behrens Adamson, took up his post in June 1904. The last locomotives delivered to the Maryport & Carlisle Railway were a pair of 0-6-0 good engines, Nos. 29 and 30, ordered from the Yorkshire Engine Co. in Sheffield. Supplied in 1921, these engines were little more than a year old when passing into LMS stock at the Grouping. They had 5ft 0in. diameter driving wheels, with a boiler pressure of 170lb. Employing Stephenson valve gear, these locomotives had 19in. x 26in. cylinders and weighed in at a hefty 49 tons 12 cwt. With a tractive effort of 22,600lb., they were, by a significant margin, the most powerful locomotives in the history of the Maryport & Carlisle Railway. However, Nos. 29 and 30 did not enjoy longevity. Having been renumbered by the LMS, No. 12513 (29) was the first to succumb in 1933. Upon the withdrawal of No. 12514 (30) the following year, the last of the Maryport & Carlisle Railway locomotives was laid to rest.

There had been a eight year break since a brand new locomotive entered service on the railway prior to receipt of North British Locomotive Co.-built 0-6-0 No. 18 in 1908.

John Alsop Collection

The most powerful Maryport & Carlisle Railway locomotives were the final pair. These were 0-6-0s Nos. 29 and 30, delivered by the Yorkshire Engine Co. in 1921. No. 30 was the last M&CR locomotive to enter traffic and the last to be withdrawn.

Author's Collection

Rolling stock

In 1845 the railway's rolling stock amounted to eight locomotives, 21 passenger vehicles and 230 wagons. On 17th February, 1857 the *Cumberland Pacquet, and Ware's Whitehaven Advertiser* reported in an audit of Maryport & Carlisle rolling stock that there were,

> 4 first class, 8 second class, 12 third class, and 1 composite carriages, 7 luggage and break vans, 3 horse boxes; 4 carriage trucks; 19 cattle trucks; 113 goods and other trucks; 20 coke trucks; 482 coal waggons; and 13 locomotive engines.

In 1912 the rolling stock was recorded as 28 locomotives, 56 items of passenger stock and some 1,667 goods vehicles. By 1922 there were 28 tender engines, five tank engines, 77 passenger vehicles, 1,480 goods vehicles and 73 service vehicles.

Remarkably a six-wheel five-compartment third, No. 11, built for the Maryport & Carlisle in 1875 by the Metropolitan Carriage & Wagon Co. survives. It was sold to the Cannock & Rugeley Colliery Co. in Staffordshire in 1922 and used to transport miners from Hednesford to Cannock Wood pit, in what was known locally as the 'Paddy Train'. The colliery company was nationalised and integrated into the National Coal Board in 1946. The former Maryport coach remained in service at the colliery until 1954, when it was left to stand in sidings at Rawnsley.

M&CR No. 11 along with an ex-Great Eastern Railway 6-wheel coach of 1894 vintage, both in derelict condition, were donated by the National Coal Board to the Railway Preservation Society (West Midlands District), the forerunner of the Chasewater Railway. They were with the preservationists at their site at Hednesford by 1960. The Maryport coach was restored and featured in the Stockton & Darlington Railway 150th anniversary event which took place at Shildon in 1975. The vehicle remains on the Chasewater Railway, where it is once more undergoing restoration.

Liveries

Locomotives were painted green. Ernest Carter, in *Britain's Railway Liveries*, states that in 1897 they had 'black bands lined on both sides with vermilion'. By 1900 Carter records the green as very similar to Great Western Railway livery, but 'edged with black lining with a fine white line outside it and a vermilion one within'.

Carter describes the carriage livery in 1895 as painted to represent red teak, and that some vehicles lasted in this livery on local services between Bullgill and Workington until 1912. In 1901 he describes the carriage livery as varnished natural teak colour. A significant change to passenger stock livery was noted in 1905, when the teak was replaced with dark green lower panels and white upper panels with gold lining around the panels and windows.

Goods stock was painted dark grey and lettered in white.

M&CR bogie tricomposite carriage No. 15. *John Alsop Collection*

The preserved 6-wheel third class coach No. 11, a 5-compartment third of 1875. The coach is being prepared for transportation from the Chasewater Railway to Shildon for the Rail 150, Stockton & Darlington Railway anniversary celebrations in 1975.
Mike Wood/Chasewater Railway Collection

Appendix One

Opening sequence of the Maryport & Carlisle

1840	Wednesday, 15th July	Maryport to the coal pits of Arkleby and Oughterside.
1841	Monday, 12th April	Arkleby pit to Aspatria. Just over a mile in length.
1843	Wednesday, 3rd May	Wigton to Carlisle.
1845	Monday, 10th February	Aspatria to Wigton.
1866	Monday, 2nd April	Bolton Loop.
1867	Saturday, 1st June (fully open)	Derwent branch.

Appendix Two

Locomotive Superintendents

1848	George Scott
1854-1870	George Tosh
1870-1878	Hugh Smellie
1878-1893	Robert Campbell
1893-1898	William Robinson
1898-1904	William Coulthard
1904-1922	John Behrens Adamson

M&CR 0-4-2 No. 4 departs Carlisle Citadel with a Maryport train in September 1912.
John Alsop Collection

Appendix Three

Opening and closure dates to passengers

Station	Opened	Closed
Initial line		
Maryport	Monday 10th February, 1845 (fully)	Still open
Dearham Bridge	Monday 10th February, 1845 (fully)	Monday 5th June, 1950
Bullgill	Monday 10th February, 1845 (fully)	Monday 7th March, 1960
Arkleby	Monday 10th February, 1845 (fully)	Thursday 1st January, 1852
Aspatria	Monday 12th April, 1841	Still open
Brayton	Private - opened in 1845	
	Public - from March 1848	Monday 5th June, 1950
Leegate	Wednesday 2nd February, 1848	Monday 5th June, 1950
Brookfield	Monday 2nd December, 1844	Monday 10th February, 1845
Wigton	Wednesday 10th May, 1843	Still open
Micklethwaite	Date unknown	June 1845
Crofton	Private station	
Curthwaite	Wednesday, 10th May, 1843	Monday 12th June, 1950
Dalston	Wednesday, 10th May, 1843	Still open
Cummersdale	October 1858	Monday 18th June, 1951
Bogfield, Carlisle	Wednesday 10th May, 1843	December 1844
Crown St, Carlisle	Monday 30th December, 1844	Saturday 17th March, 1849
The Bolton Loop		
Baggrow	Wednesday 26th December, 1866	Monday 22nd September, 1930
Mealsgate	Wednesday 26th December, 1866	Monday 22nd September, 1930
High Blaithwaite	Tuesday 1st October, 1878	Monday 1st August, 1921
The Derwent Branch		
Dearham	Saturday 1st June, 1867	Monday 29th April, 1935
Linefoot	Tuesday 1st September, 1908	Sunday 1st November, 1908
Dovenby Lodge	Private station	
Papcastle	Saturday 1st June, 1867	Friday 1st July, 1921
[Brigham – Joint]	Wednesday 28th April, 1847	Monday 18th April, 1966

For closures the date given is the first day the service was withdrawn.

An undated view of Maryport station looking northwards. *G. Biddle Collection/Kidderminster Railway Museum*

Sources and thanks

Parliamentary Acts
Railway Record
Herepath's Journal
Milner's Guide to Railways Coaches and Steamers in the North of England
The British Steam Railway Locomotive 1825 to 1925, E.L. Ahrons, Locomotive Publishing Co., 1927
The Maryport & Carlisle Railway, Jack Simmons, Oakwood Press (OL4), 1947
Locomotives at the Grouping No. 3 London Midland & Scottish Railway,
   H.C Casserley & S.W. Johnson, Ian Allan, 1966
Britain's Railway Liveries 1825-1948, Ernest F. Carter, Third Edition, Harold Starke Ltd, 1980
British Steam Locomotive Builders, James W. Lowe, 1975
The Solway Junction Railway, Stuart Edgar & John M. Sinton, Oakwood Press (LP176), 1990
Clinker's Register of closed passenger stations and goods depots in England, Scotland and Wales 1830-1980, C.R. Clinker, Avon Anglia, 1980

Newspapers sourced through the British Newspaper Archive:

Carlisle Journal
Carlisle Patriot
Carlisle Express and Examiner
Carlisle Nationalist
Maryport Advertiser
Workington Star
Whitehaven News
Wigton Advertiser
Westmorland Gazette
West Cumberland Times
Penrith Observer
The English Lakes Visitor
Soulby's Ulverston Advertiser and General Intelligence
The Scotsman
Edinburgh Evening News
Leeds Mercury
Derby Mercury

The line is mentioned, it seems, only once in the *Bucks Herald – Uxbridge Advertiser – Windsor and Eton Journal*. It reports on 14th January, 1860 that,

A 'brisk damsel' had boarded a train at Dalston. She was wearing a circular appendage to her dress and on attempting to alight at Dearham it caught in the carriage handle and she was suspended in mid-air. The guard came to her rescue and on being freed she made a quick exit from the scene'.

Thanks

To Ian Kennedy who turned the manuscript into a book and sourced photographs, plans and maps.
   To Russ Rollings for his meticulous proof reading.
   This railway had, for its size, more than what was usually the number of Parliamentary Acts and the help of the staff at the House of Lords Record Office in sorting these is very much appreciated.

Index

Abbey, 53
Abbey Holme, 9, 16
Accidents, 15, 59, 69, 80
Acts of Parliament, 9 et seq., 16 et seq., 23, 32, 37, 42 et seq., 45 et seq., 52 et seq.
Adamson & Co., 54
Adamson, John Behrens, 65, 113
Addison, John, 50, 59, 63
Aikbank Junction, 54, 57, 60, 71, 75, 82, 91
Allhallows, 54, 91, 92
Allonby, 50
Allport, James, 35
Arkleby, 12 et seq., 41, 43, 45
Aspatria, 14, 16, 19, 23, 24, 25, 27, 28, 41, 45, 47, 49, 50, 51, 55, 81, 84, 85, 91
Baggrow, 58, 91, 92, 93
Barns, G.H., 28
Barton & Tweddle, 23
Beyer, Peacock, & Co., 61, 106, 107, 109, 113
Birkby, 11
Blackmore, John, 12, 14, 15, 17
Blackstock & McKay, 12, 23
Blain, Thomas, 65
Blaydon, 6, 30
Bolton Loop, 53 et seq., 60, 63, 81, 82, 84, 90 et seq.
Botchergate, 19, 43
Brayton, 41, 49, 72, 81, 83
Brigham, 55, 57, 59, 97
Brookfield, 23, 75
Broughton Cross, 58
Broughton Moor, 51
Bullgill, 41, 55, 58, 59, 81, 86, 95, 115
Caledonian Rly, 31 et seq., 43
Campbell, Robert, 61
Carlisle,
  Bogfield, 16, 17, 19, 21, 31, 38, 43
  Canal, 50
  Citadel, 31 et seq., 40, 43, 45, 50, 54, 74 et seq.
  Crown Street, 17, 19, 21, 24, 26, 30 et seq., 35, 38, 43, 69, 76
  Currock, 61, 67, 68, 74, 75, 108
  London Road, 16, 17, 31, 33, 45
Carlisle, Annan & Liverpool Steam Co., 31
Carnforth, 51
Carr, Hugh, 63
Chasewater Railway, 115, 116
Cleator & Workington Junction Rly, 94, 95
Coat of Arms, 11
Cockermouth, 17, 51, 57, 59
Cockermouth & Workington Rly, 48, 55, 57, 59
Cockermouth, Keswick & Penrith Rly, 57, 63
Coddrington, Capt., 23
Coulthard, William, 63
Cowan, William, 35, 36

Crampton locomotives, 99, 100
Craven, G., 16
Croall, Henderson & Fearon, 19
Crofton, 75, 79
Crosby, 55, 81
Cummersdale, 15, 50, 75, 77
Curthwaite, 41, 47, 49, 75, 79
Dalston, 7, 16, 41, 49, 50, 51, 75, 78
Dearham, 59, 94, 95
Dearham Bridge, 21, 41, 49, 51, 69, 71, 81, 87
Dees, John, 47
Derwent branch, 55, 86, 94 et seq., 111, 112
Dividends, 7, 14, 21, 24, 27, 30, 35, 39, 45, 47, 48, 51, 55, 61, 63, 65, 69, 71, 73
Dovenby Lodge, 58, 63, 95
Dübs & Co., 113
Dykes, F.L.B., 13, 15 et seq., 19, 24, 30, 34
Dykes, Mrs Ballantine, 59, 95
Gilcrux, 12, 14
Glasgow & South Western Rly, 61, 74, 75, 105
Grouping, The, 5, 73
Hall, William Snooke, 6, 7, 9
Harrington, 25, 26
Harris, John, 28
Harrison, George, 36, 45
Hartlepool Rly, 99
Hartley, G.W., 36, 39, 61
Hartley, Thomas, 65
Hawthorn & Co., 15, 49, 98, 99
Hexham, 6
Heysham, T.C., 28, 32
High Blaithwaite, 55, 58, 71, 90, 91
Hudson, George, 28 et seq., 48
Ireland, 7, 24, 26, 31
Irving, William, 14
Jacob, Henry, 34, 36, 39, 40, 47
Kendal, 13
Keswick, 51
Kirtlebridge, Annan & Brayton Rly, 81
Kitson, Robert, 11
Lancaster, 12
Lancaster & Carlisle Rly, 19, 21, 26, 27, 31 et seq., 38, 43, 45, 57
Lawson, Sir Wilfrid, 7, 9, 61, 63, 75
Leegate, 41, 49, 75, 82
Linefoot, 65, 94, 95
Livery, 65, 115
Locomotives, 2, 12 et seq., 23, 24, 47, 49, 68, 74, 76, 78, 89, 98 et seq.
London, Midland & Scottish Rly (LMS), 5, 73, 102 et seq., 107 et seq., 109, 111 et seq.
London & North Western Rly (LNWR), 57, 58, 74, 88, 95, 97
Lonsdale, Lord, 30
Low Row, 23, 75
Lyndall, Joseph, 47, 50
Marron Foot, 57

Marron Junction, 59
Maryport,
  Docks, 38, 48, 67, 81, 88, 89
  Station, 57, 81, 88, 89, 118
Mealsgate, 53 et seq., 58, 91
Metropolitan Carriage & Wagon Co., 115, 116
Micklethwaite, 118
Midland Rly, 29, 35, 57
Mitchell, William, 13, 19, 21, 28
Mounsey, G.C., 15, 26, 28, 36, 37
Namur & Liege Rly, 100
Neilson, Reid, & Co., 110, 111, 113
North Eastern Rly, 54, 57
Newcastle & Berwick Rly, 29
Newcastle & Carlisle Rly, 6 et seq., 12, 16, 17, 19, 22, 28, 29, 31, 33, 38, 43, 45, 48, 54, 74, 98
North British Locomotive Co., 65, 113, 114
Oughterside, 12 et seq., 81
Paisley, General, 15
Papcastle, 58, 95, 96
Penrith, 13, 51
Rae, Dr, 11
Richardson, Thomas, & Sons, 99
Robinson, William, 63, 111
Rolling stock, 115, 116
Rosegill, 59, 81
Sale, S.H., 28, 34
Senhouse, Capt. Sir Humphrey le Fleming, 6, 9, 11, 63
Senhouse, J.P., 7, 14, 15, 81
Shares, 7 et seq., 17, 26 et seq., 43, 47, 48, 63, 69
Sharp, Stewart & Co., 49, 100, 101, 113
Silloth, 47, 48, 50
Smellie, William, 60, 61, 105, 109
Solway Junction Rly, 81, 83
Staveling Stone, 9
Stephenson, George, 6 et seq., 12
Stockton & Darlington Rly, 98, 115, 116
Swift & Co., 32
Timetables, 19, 24 et seq., 40, 41, 46, 47, 49, 50, 62, 66, 69, 71
Tosh, George, 45, 47, 54, 60, 101, 105
Tulk & Ley, 13, 49, 98 et seq.
Whitehaven, 8, 12, 17, 19, 51, 58, 88
Wigton, 7, 9, 14 et seq., 23 et seq., 40, 41, 46, 47, 49, 51, 54, 61, 63, 64, 69 et seq., 75, 80
Wilson, E.B., & Co., 49, 100
Wood, John, 11
Workington, 17, 94, 115
World War I, 71, 73
York & Newcastle Rly, 29
York, Berwick & Carlisle Rly, 33
York, Newcastle & Berwick Rly, 29, 30, 34, 38, 99
Yorkshire Engine Co., 65, 101, 113, 114